QUEENOLOGY
There's A Queen Inside Of You

R.C. BLAKES, JR.

Published by Untapped Potential Publishing
P.O. Box 571083 Houston, TX 77257

UNTAPPED POTENTIAL
PUBLISHING

CONTENTS

FOREWORD

A queen? Who me? No, not me. Do you know who I am, what I've been through, the pain I've gone through, the misery and shame I've endured? Queen? No, not me.

This was my way of thinking not that long ago. I knew no other way. My self-esteem was literally below zero on a scale of 1-10.

My grandmother had been abused and broken, my mother had been abused and broken, and I am no exception—yes, I have been abused and broken! Can a broken woman be a queen? How can she rise up from the ashes and tap into the queen inside?

As I lay in my room March 8, 2017, all I could do was weep! On that day, I reached the golden age of 50. Reflecting over my life, the tears flowed uncontrollably. Even as I write this, the tears are flowing. You may wonder why.

You see, the vision I saw for my life was shallow. It did not include a fraction of the life I currently live. I could not see myself married with children, much less having grandchildren. I did not believe I would ever be happy. In my head, I was supposed to be dead a long time ago. In fact, I tried to end my life on a few occasions.

But God's plan and purpose overruled.

He allowed a man of God, R.C. Blakes to find me. The rest is history. Well, the Word of God says, "*He that findeth a wife, findeth a good thing . . .*"

Wow, I sometimes wonder if R.C. got short-changed. He found a wife all right, but one that was a mess. Broken to the very core! What I didn't know was that God had fully equipped this man, my husband, to bring healing and restoration to a broken queen. He allowed him to:

1. See and know that his good thing was broken.
2. Learn how to put his good thing back together.
3. Empower his good thing.

The journey has not been easy. The process has required a lot of work. The information my husband shares in this book are the very principles he used to repair his broken queen. Learning how to manage my emotions and how to overcome my insecurities and negativity had to be the toughest challenges. A well-equipped king with much love and patience has put this queen on her throne! I thank God for my king because now I reign!

If you are a king with the desire to empower a queen, or a queen who is rising from the ashes, this book is for you. It is my prayer that every woman will find the queen inside her and begin to live the life she is destined to live.

—LISA BLAKES

INTRODUCTION

This book is the sequel to another book I wrote called *The Father Daughter Talk*. Within these pages we will look at the process of renewing the woman's mind from an unconscious inferior and victim to a queen-consciousness. Despite the world's best efforts to miniaturize the woman's self-definition, the present message is that *you are a queen*, regardless of life's challenges.

The obvious question is: what is "queenology?" When we look at the word in its two parts (*queen-ology*), the meaning becomes clear.

Typically, a *queen* is a female ruler or monarch. She is a dignitary of the highest order with power and the consciousness to execute that power.

The suffix *-ology* refers to the study of something. For instance, *theology* is the study of God, *psychology* is the study of the mind, and *sociology* is the study of people.

Queenology is the study of queens!

My mission is to awaken the ruler within generations of women who are presently anesthetized. This is not another brand of feminism; rather, this is kingdom order. God created women to dominate. Our mothers, wives, sisters, and daughters are to dominate the earth and to reign over amazing lives. As I discuss in *The Father Daughter Talk*, many women have been stymied by fatherless homes and manipulative men. The personal perspective of most women has been broken. *Queenology* is my way of saying: broken or not, *you are still queen!*

> *A queen is the quintessential woman possessing the ultimate presence and excellent character, empowered by a no-nonsense approach to life, love, and business.*

The one and only Bishop T.D. Jakes once presented a most powerful illustration. He took a crisp one hundred dollar bill and asked the audience, "What is the value of this bill?" The response was, "One hundred dollars." He then dropped the bill to the floor and stepped on it. He picked it up and asked, "What is the value of this bill?" The response was, "One hundred dollars." Then he crumpled the bill, and when he was done abusing it, he unfolded it and asked, "What is the value of this bill?" The response once again was, "One hundred dollars." Bishop Jakes then went off of the rails and actually tore the bill into two pieces, you could hear the audience gasp for breath. He then took some clear tape and put the pieces together. Once again he asked, "Now what is the value of this bill?" The resounding response was, *"One hundred dollars!"* At that point, you could see the tears of the broken begin to flow. They caught a most powerful revelation that day. *Queenology* is my attempt to help put the pieces back together again. It's my way of saying: you are still queen, you can still reign, and here is how.

*It matters not what you've been through in
life, your identity and value are unchanged by
your circumstances. You are still a queen.*

Through these pages we will move from pain to power, defeat to conquest. My intent is to reprogram the parts of the queen's self-view that have been fractured by unfair circumstances, untrue female inferiority propaganda, and the unfortunate absence of certain vital influences in her life. My goal is to reset the mentality and thereby elevate the behavior to that which becomes a queen. I like to call this kind of enlightenment *queen-consciousness*. Something shifts when a woman embodies the revelation that she is a queen.

*A queen must know that she is a queen
before she can function as such.*

I believe that there is something deeply prophetic about me, as a man, striving to restore spiritual and psychological balance to the way women think. After all, generations of men have plundered the self-esteem bank of women. There's something powerful when men rise up to remind women of who they really are versus what she has been indoctrinated to believe. There is often a vast difference between what you've been indoctrinated to believe about yourself versus the truth of who you are. All marginalized people are led by the controlling powers to think less of themselves than they should.

*The difference between kings and queens
versus slaves and beggars is an awareness
of true personal worth and power.*

I believe that this is a point in human history where God will continue to raise up men to restore the honor to women. I have often been accused of breaking what some call the "man code" because I teach women how to recognize relational games and to avoid the psychological traps that certain men perpetuate upon a gullible female population. When I am posed with such accusations, I use the occasion to educate the misguided brothers. The first mark of a real man is an insatiable desire to protect womanhood. A real man does not seek to break her, he works to build her. Furthermore, any real "man code" cannot avoid the "father code." A real man would want to do nothing to any woman he wouldn't want done against his own daughter. He should freely communicate to any woman willing to listen the same knowledge concerning the world that he would share with his daughter.

Kings produce queens.

As a biological father of three young women, I have always endeavored to communicate their royalty through my words and deeds. There has always been something within me that recognized my role in cementing their *queen-con-sciousness*. As their father, I realized I could diminish their self-perspective or I could magnify it. I chose to expand my girls' self-view. As a consequence, I am currently the proud father of three beautiful *black queens*! One is an educator and principal, another is a business woman, and the third is presently double-majoring at DePaul University.

On a deeper level, I am married to a beautiful *caribbean queen*! I call her "Lee," which is short for Lisa. My wife is saved, beautiful, powerful, educated, and a woman reaching for her own goals. She is my greatest support and the love of my life. However, her present life does not reflect the journey she's taken. She looks nothing like the hell she's lived through.

The Story of a Broken Queen
(Lisa's story)

As a very small child, Lisa was separated from her beloved mother by her abusive father. She was brought from Jamaica to Canada. While in Canada, she was abused in horrendous ways. It was so bad that by the age of sixteen she emancipated herself and ran away. She worked, went to school, and took sole responsibility for her own well-being. She was alone and without any support system. That still makes me sad.

At the same time that she was exuding so much strength for a young girl, her self-esteem had been so depleted that she had no concept of self-worth. She went through seasons of suicidal thoughts. The queen that she was was eclipsed by a cloud of human depravity; but despite all that she suffered, she was nonetheless *queen.*

A queen is a queen either sitting on a throne, beautifully arrayed, or broken in the gutter. Her value and identity are immutable.

A crown is no less valuable because it's been fractured, and a woman is no less queen because she's been broken.

My love for Lisa made me do something I had never done before—*I paid attention.* Sometimes I would get extremely frustrated with her behavior and weird ways. She was too possessive, always suspicious, and uncomfortable with compliments. As I paid attention, I learned how to love a broken queen. It was extremely frustrating for me to see her as a queen and to realize that she was completely oblivious to her own power.

It was through patience, consistency, stability, and honesty that I earned her trust. Once that happened, I could then begin to teach her who she really was. I was teaching her even when she didn't realize it. I remember the first time she prepared a meal for me. She brought it to me and I said thank you. She was amazed that I articulated appreciation for her kindness. At that point, I realized that I was not just being polite, I was being used by God to reset her personal self-esteem. She began to learn her worth and would soon demand it.

The next lesson was for her to allow me, as her man, to open doors for her. Sometimes we still struggle with this lesson. The point is, as her man I have intentionally exposed her to her true worth and identity. I am teaching my wife that she is a *queen*! She treats me like a king because I honor her as queen.

Sometimes a woman develops her queen-consciousness in her husband's care.

I am so glad that the Lord chose me as Lisa's husband to help tape the pieces of her broken soul back together again. Today, decades later, she declares her own worth, knows her true power, and demands acknowledgment of her value. She has come a million miles from the broken little princess she used to be. She is a full-grown queen now, and the mother of queens across America, boldly declaring her worth and exuding the essence of royalty. Of course, this is totally God's doing. I am just elated to have been an instrument in this process. She will write her own story one day.

In the pages that follow, we will discuss how a queen thinks and behaves from her conscious place of power. When you have purged the pain and slave-conditioning from your mind, you must awaken to your true identity and accept the call to live as the queen you are.

There are many uncomfortable and challenging adjustments that may be required of you as we take this journey into your queen-consciousness. Just as the biblical character Esther trusted the council of Mordecai, resulting in her ruling as queen, I ask that you test and trust the wisdom that I will share with you.

Once again, this is as a father speaking to the heart of his daughter—it's a king speaking to a queen to simply remind you of your heritage and your destiny. The intent is to shift your self-definition and your idea of what is possible and acceptable for you.

YOU ARE A QUEEN.

THE QUEEN

by Jan K. Thomas

*I'm speaking to the bruised and broken
woman who feels like she's fallen apart.*

*I'm speaking to the fearful and abused to
restore music to the silenced heart.*

*I'm speaking to the insecure and forgotten
whose father acted like she didn't exist.*

*To the ones weakened and who have
lost hope—you are also on my list.*

*Don't let anyone diminish your instinct to
love, nurture, and care. For you are so much
more than your nails, makeup, and hair.*

*You have developed spiritual amnesia and you have
forgotten who you are. You have let your pain overtake
you, I remind you there's strength in your scar.*

*You will no longer be a victim—you have inherited
a life you've not yet seen. Lift up your head and
adjust your crown, for you, my dear, are a queen.*

*Discovering your own personal truth will inspire you
and make you free. Embrace your identity in God's
love and light, not who you were told you would be.*

*Put on your robe of magnificence stand in your
moment as pure gold. You are unaware of your royal
bloodline and are asleep to the power you hold.*

*Awaken to your destiny and purpose—God chose
you for life to pass through. Mary birthed the Word
of God, Jesus, what answers will be birthed in you?*

*The voice of your past and society wants you to believe
that you are less because you have emotions and
intuition and might choose to wear heels or a dress.*

*Embrace your womanhood to the fullest, being
female is not being cursed. Your race has already been*

determined—as it is written, the last shall be first.

The prison of your personal pain can make your heart grow silent and cold. How can you fully reign, your Highness, if you are still being controlled?

You are worth far more than any jewel, no one could ever take your place. You were designed by God as an original, blessed to conquer whatever you face.

You are a fierce protector of your beloved, your seed will crush evil's head. Your rival is only yourself, your babies fulfill what you've said.

Your touch waters empty souls, your voice encourages us to thrive. Arise now and take your rightful place, we need our queens to survive.

You are fire, the rock, the rose, and the stream. You are the hope, the truth, the lotus, and the dream.

Get ready to walk in the path you've not seen. You are royalty and power.

YOU ARE QUEEN.

Prologue

Indulge me in my attempt at a prologue. It is the fictional tale of King Paternam and his three daughters Princess Honestum, Princess Imperium, and Princess Potestatum. I will attempt to weave the story of the king and his daughters throughout the book, as their story will correlate to the principles and wisdom I will convey in these pages.

King Paternam discovers that he has to take the social and psychological development of his daughters into his own hands due to some unforeseen challenges. The king employs a very specific process to create a very specific mindset—the mindset of queens. The king desires to establish a queen's consciousness within his girls. From chapter to chapter we will briefly revisit their story.

QUEEN-CONSCIOUSNESS
(The King and the Three Princesses)

Once upon a time, in a land not too far away, there was a king by the name of Paternam. King Paternam had three beautiful daughters—Honestum, Imperium, and Potes-tatem. The king had been at war for many years which had taken him on a long journey. While King Paternam was away, Queen Materno, his wife and the mother of his girls, died. After her death and his absence, there was no regal presence to train the very young princesses. The girls were left in the hands of those who miseducated them and indoctrinated them against their royal identity. The court and the subjects abused the young regals because of their lack of self-knowledge and the absence of their kingly father's presence.

> When a queen is miseducated, her
> power may be easily usurped.

Upon the king's sudden and unexpected return, he discovered these young queens were totally oblivious to their potential and place in the kingdom. They knew nothing of their true status. They were royalty, yet they behaved as commoners. They were insecure around those who were really servants to them, controlled by those who were actually subjects. They were begging for what already belonged to them, and they set their goals far beneath the thrones for which they were born.

The king's first action was to behead those who miseducated the young queens. His second action was to sit his daughters down and train them in the ways of queens.

Though the king's kingdom was still in a state of disarray and many issues needed attention, he put no agenda ahead of training the young princesses. He began by un-teaching the lies they learned about being inferior, powerless, unattractive, and limited. He taught them who they were, what they possessed, the power they had, the future they should expect, and the qualities of a man who would qualify to be their king. King Paternam worked on the mentality of his daughters for years until one day they walked, talked, and thought like the queens they were born to be. The king called this course of study Queenology.

QUEENS MANAGE EMOTIONS

QUEEN-CONSIOUSNESS
(Emotional Instability May Cost You the Kingdom)

As the king started re-training his daughters, he noticed that their deeply embedded insecurities and doubts were playing out on the canvas of their emotional lives. The girls were extremely emotional and reactive. This grieved the king because he knew that it was not the temperament of queens.

As a result, one of the very first lessons King Paternam taught his young princesses was that queens may not wear their thoughts and emotions on their shoulders. Rulers don't react. The king said, "A queen will never be moved by words or circumstances. A queen is never emotional—she is always intentional and measured."

The king said, "One cannot effectively strategize against a plot if her thoughts and feelings are obvious through unbridled emotion.

"A queen is more strategic than emotional. One badly placed emotional outburst or meltdown can cost a queen her reputation, respect, and possibly her throne."

As the young girls listened to the wisdom of their father and thought about their ways, it was clear that the lesson was being taken to heart.

There's nothing more dangerous than being a woman who is emotionally out of control. The world will toy with this woman like a puppet. As a pastor, I have seen women destroy their homes, dismantle marriages, and cripple their promising careers, all because they were emotionally unstable. I've seen unscrupulous men take advantage of women simply because they were driven by their emotions and not their intellect or spiritual discernment. Average women are emotionally unstable. Powerful women harness their emotional impulses.

A queen works hard at managing her emotions.

A queen is a woman of the highest nobility, character, affluence, and influence. Her station in life demands self-discipline. A queen cannot be the standard for a nation, daughter, wife, or mother of kings and simultaneously meltdown in the mall because somebody got her parking space. Her position calls for patience, confidence, calm, and poise when others are everything but. A queen does not show her hand. She is calm in a storm.

A queen is the most powerful woman and carries greater responsibility. She must possess a corresponding temperament. She can't afford to be emotionally exposed.

As female rulers of the age, queens have no space for the typical emotional instability that average women demonstrate. In modern urban vernacular, the queen is the *boss*. A boss recognizes that she is responsible for much, and too many people stand on her shoulders for her to be an emotional thermometer. A thermometer simply displays the temperature without any control over it. When a woman is emotionally undisciplined, she simply displays whatever emotion the moment dictates, even when it is to her own peril. Queens must never be emotional thermometers; rather, queens must be the emotional thermostat that establishes the temperature in every situation.

A queen can't be unstable!

Emotions are too capricious *(inconsistent)* to be allowed to control your life. They should never control the woman; the woman must control her emotions. Uncontrolled emotions are like a runaway train destroying everything in its path, coming to the tragic end of itself. Many women have destroyed relationships, careers, and friendships because of their lack of emotional discipline.

Women are socially conditioned to believe that they must be emotionally unstable because they are female. This is a blatant deception!

The modern woman too frequently buys in to the myth that she has no choice but to be on a temperamental roller coaster. She believes that she has no capacity to control her emotions and will always be emotionally frantic. Consequently some women live lives of instability and chaos. The idea that a woman is always incapable of balancing her emotions is clearly a blatant lie.

Powerful women throughout history have proven that a determined woman can conquer her emotions—Queen Esther, Harriet Tubman, Oprah Winfrey, Hillary Clinton, and Michelle Obama all stayed cool under some of the greatest emotional, social, and psychological pressure. Great women always disprove the myth by being level-headed and even-tempered under pressure.

How would you describe your emotional maturity as a woman? Are you reactionary or responsive?

I remember so vividly when Hillary Clinton ignored the public pressure to leave her husband after the horrific scandal during Mr. Clinton's presidency. She overrode obvious feelings of embarrassment and hurt to keep her family and their political legacy intact. If she had been a woman given to acting on momentary impulses, the story would have been quite different. Mrs. Clinton later ran for, but did not win, the 2016 Presidential election; however, she won the popular vote by nearly three-million votes. She proved to be an emotionally strong and equivalent leader.

The world says that women are by nature
too emotional for serious responsibility.

When a woman is emotionally unregulated, she feeds the false and antiquated belief that women can't lead or manage others. The world wants her to believe that she can't control her emotions, so she may be discredited at every opportunity and passed over for advancement. The world will give a woman an opportunity and sit by quietly, waiting for her to implode. When she has the anticipated meltdown, the world will strip her of her power. The premise is that if a woman can't be in control of herself, she can't be responsible for others or the caretaker of great power.

Also, when a woman has no emotional control, she is socially and relationally vulnerable. She is compromised by her own emotions.

Emotion is a clear window into the soul.

The Bible declares in Proverbs 25:28, *He who has no rule over his own spirit is like a city that is broken down and without walls* (AMPC). The message of the text indicates that a person who does not learn to control her feelings and emotions is defenseless.

> *A queen cannot afford to be emotionally predisposed because enemies will use her exposed emotions to compromise her power.*

It is extremely unwise for a woman to reveal her emotions to people who have not proven their love for or commitment to protect her. It is frightening to witness women expose themselves emotionally to people they don't even know. To share your deepest feelings with a man you've only recently met is dangerous, to say the least. It is even perilous for a woman to be too emotional with other unproven women.

> *Would a woman expose her naked body to people she does not know intimately? Not normally. Likewise, a queen clothes her naked emotions in the garment of self-control.*

A queen understands this fact: if she is not in control of her emotions, someone else is. I remember the early days of my pastorate. I would come to church and wonder why the temperature in the sanctuary would fluctuate frequently from hot to cold. Finally, one of the deacons pointed out that the thermostats were exposed to anyone who desired to change them, and the members would change the temperature at will. We had to put lock boxes over the thermostats to maintain control of the environment. The lesson I learned from that experience was that a thermostat should not be exposed to the general public.

Likewise, a woman must not give the world access to her emotional thermostat. She will not have control of herself as long as she is emotionally accessible to everybody. A powerful woman will always be in control of her emotions.

A weak woman doesn't even try to manage her own emotions. She allows circumstances and other people to establish the condition of her spiritual and psychological temperature.

> *If you don't have control of your emotions,*
> *someone else does. When you're out of*
> *control, someone else is in control.*

When you protect your emotions, you own your personal power and can dictate the atmosphere around you. Once your emotions are on unbridled display, your life may be managed by less intelligent people.

> *The genius who is emotionally unstable will*
> *serve the idiot who has control of his emotions.*

Have you ever asked yourself how a loud, old, ignorant, and tasteless pervert of a man can convince a young beautiful woman to prostitute her body while he takes her money? The women are carefully chosen from a particular profile—they target young women who have abuse in their backgrounds and are so emotionally traumatized they wear their feelings on their sleeves. These men move in and begin to manipulate the woman with her own words and reactions. Her emotions signify what she wants, feels, needs, and most desires. The predator manipulates her until she is caught in a trap she can't escape from.

A woman cannot master her emotions
when her thoughts are rooted in negative
past experiences like abuse, betrayal,
and other psychological wounding.

One of the major problems with women who are emotionally unpredictable is that they have not completely processed their pain. Such a woman may have a history of unfortunate and undeserved infractions against her that have left her emotionally broken. Her soul is broken and can't contain her moment-to-moment feelings or thoughts. She is like a cracked vase that can't contain water—as much as she tries, the water still seems to escape.

The residue of pain generates an environment of emotional chaos. The thoughts she thinks will create her emotions.

As a queen, you must understand that
continuing to live in your dark past will
consistently sabotage your destiny.

Unprocessed pain always creeps into the future to perpetuate even greater damage than the original impact. Hebrews 12:15 says to watch out for this, *lest any root of bitterness springing up trouble you, and thereby many be defiled.* The point of this text is that the bitterness of pain eventually defiles everything it contacts. Pain doesn't simply go away, it must be put away.

The woman's intent focus on past negativity is often

the cause of the attitude and behavior that dismantles opportunities and prevents progress. She is emotionally out of sync because her thoughts are backwards.

How does a queen conquor emotions?
She must consciously establish her
own emotional expectations.

A queen must establish emotional expectations of herself. In other words, predetermine how you will respond to scenarios before they occur. Plan for every scenario imaginable and predetermine how you will respond to it. Average women react, queens respond. For instance, if your mother-in-law always pushes your button about your cooking and you react emotionally, you may spark an argument between you and your husband for a week. Instead, predetermine a wise response to her negativity. Take control of the moment. Don't fall to the expectations and manipulation of others; rise to your own higher expectations of yourself. You are not out of control and less than a leader. You are a wise, brilliant, and composed woman!

Live your life from the inside out, which is the highest perspective. People who live from their spirit are never managed by external conditions. Whatever is present in your soul and spirit will manifest on the canvas of your life.

A great biblical principle teaches us to establish
our thinking and our lives will follow.

Proverbs 23:7 declares: *As he thinketh in his heart, so is he.* The message of the text is this: whatever you want to project to others, you must produce it internally first. *You will always be as you think. Being follows conceiving.* When you can conceive yourself as a powerful queen who is always emotionally solid, your reality will be as you see it.

A queen must study other women who thrive in high pressure environments.

Every woman should identify other women who are models of stability and strength. At a certain point, you need to see a person who shares your experiences and chemistry and models your desired standard. We all need mentors. Mentors are sometimes up close and personal while at other times are at a distance. You may find mentors from the pages of history or in current books. For instance, stories of the women who beat the odds during the women's suffrage movement to pave the way for women today will inspire a woman's greatest self to surface. The Bible says that we should all follow someone who is accomplished in our aspirations.

The Bible states in Hebrews 6:12 to *be followers of them who through faith and patience inherit the promises.* One of my spiritual daughters is Carla Cannon, one of America's rising stars in the area of coaching people into entrepreneurship. Carla has a practice that will benefit all queens—she reads veraciously, mostly books by strong, successful women. Every queen needs to walk in the footsteps of queens who have gone before.

As you think about role models in your life, you may discover that your current negative condition may be the result of following the wrong examples. If you want to model a higher level of self-control, you must change the quality of women in your circle of influence. *Many queens have been dethroned because of the company they kept.* I believe that a person's environment has more of an impact on her destiny than her education or pedigree. When you surround yourself with people who are everything you want to be, you become what you want to be.

So, a queen is very intentional about her influences. She does not lend her ears or give her time to people who do not contribute to the manifestation of her best version of herself.

A queen must self-correct immediately
when her emotions start to surge.

At the end of the day you are not a robot. You will have moments when your emotions may teeter on overload, and you must be conscious enough to return to center, to emotional and spiritual balance. Get control of yourself sooner than later and return to your place of balance.

The Bible refers to this exercise as repentance. *The Complete Word Study Bible* states that repentance is a change of mind from evil to good or from good to better. Repentance is the simple act of changing your mind and correcting your course to match your new thinking. When your emotions begin to get out of hand, and they will, don't let them go the distance. Get a handle on them and turn the ship in the direction you really want to go. The Bible in 2 Corinthians 10:5 calls this casting your unprofitable thoughts down. Thoughts that are not serving your higher purpose must not be entertained. The actual text in 2 Corinthians 10:5 actually states, . . . *casting down imaginations, and every high thing that exalteth itself against the knowledge of God, and bringing into captivity every thought to the obedience of Christ.*

When our momentary thoughts don't agree with God's best plan for us, we have the responsibility to change our course by changing what we are thinking.

> *Don't allow a foolish momentary*
> *impulse to become a full-blown*
> *meltdown—recognize and reset.*

There's no shame in being human. The key is to catch your-self before you wreck yourself. Even the Lord Jesus Christ had an emotional moment right before he was to go to Calvary to suffer crucifixion. His disciples were not sup-portive and he was in great emotional agony at the very thought of suffering. The beauty is that we also see how he self-corrected and came back to his emotional center.

In Luke 22:41- 43 tells it this way:

> *And he was withdrawn from them about a*
> *stone's cast, and kneeled down, and prayed,*
> *Saying, Father, if thou be willing, remove this*
> *cup from me: nevertheless not my will, but thine*
> *be done.*

> *And there appeared an angel unto him from*
> *heaven, strengthening him.*

Jesus was experiencing the influence of fear. The beauty is that he did not allow the impulse to linger; he pulled it down. Jesus self-corrected his emotional state by feeling the emo-tion, allowing himself the moment to be human, but then quickly turning to God and the Father's will for him. As he re-submitted himself to the Father's plan, he returned to his emotional center and the angels strengthened his resolve.

When you make a choice to correct emotional instability and to be strong in the thing God has called you to, there will always be heavenly reinforcement to strengthen you.

A queen must renew her mind with God's word.

A woman must understand the spiritual dynamics behind her state of extreme emotional instability. Mental strongholds develop in the mind and these strongholds serve to cement the woman's behavior in a series of self-defeating habits. A stronghold imposes itself upon the woman against her will. She can want to do better and never find the path to change her actions, but there is always something on the inside that will try to pull her away from her best intentions.

The only way to eliminate an internal stronghold is to introduce the word of God into the soul.

This is precisely why Romans 12:2 says, *And be not conformed to this world: but be ye transformed by the renewing of your mind, that ye may prove what is that good, and acceptable, and perfect, will of God.* Transformation is the internal action of growing into all that God has predestined you to be, from the inside out. As you intake the word of God, your inner greatness emerges. The text also says that we are transformed by the "renewing" of our minds. To renew something is to restore it back to an original standard of excellence. (*The Complete Word Study Bible* says that the term renew in Romans 12:2 is the original Greek term *anakaínōsis*, which means to renew qualitatively.)

The original woman, Eve, was created to dominate; she was not a slave to anything. As a woman hears God's word and believes it, she is returned to her original place of power.

*As a woman faithfully receives the word of
God, her thinking and behavior progressively
return to the higher standards of dominion
and power that God originally intended.*

The word of God is the only source that can uproot a life-time of false beliefs and slave-conditioning imprisoning a woman through media, music, and even ministry that often suggests she is emotionally hopeless simply because she's female.

*The word of God is a queen's reference for God's
opinion of her versus the lies of the world.*

As she allows the word of God to wash over her soul, she discovers a strength she never knew she had. Rather than being driven by every emotional impulse, a queen stands on her power and inner strength as the word of God delivers her mind from the grips of instability. James 1:21 says to *receive with meekness the engrafted word, which is able to save your souls.* The term *soul* refers to the *mind, will, and emotions.* So, the word of God will deliver the woman from broken emotions. The key is to receive the word and allow it to be planted in your heart.

You can be a woman of great emotional strength. In fact, your destiny depends on it. *Rise up, queen!*

CHAPTER 2

QUEENS
STUDY
KINGS

QUEEN-CONSCIOUSNESS
(A Queen Must Be as a King, but in a Dress)

As King Paternam proceeded to train his daughters in the ways of queens, he noticed that they had been miseducated to believe that they were less than men simply because they were women. He knew this had been done to make it easier to usurp the young girls' personal and legal power. The king obliterated this concept of inferiority and naivety by affirming the girls as rulers.

*"Do you girls know the difference between a king and a queen?" he asked. "Not really," they responded. The king said, "**A queen is simply a king in a gown. She possesses the same power and strength!**" Something shifted in the eyes of the young princesses as their father drilled this idea into their heads, "**You are equal to any man** and are the rightful heirs to thrones."*

The king then gave them an assignment: He commanded the girls to observe the tendencies of men and then report back to him. He wanted the young queens to explain to him how men thought and conducted themselves in business and relationships. The king knew that they would have to be wise enough to lead a kingdom of strong men with precision, confidence, and decisiveness. How could the girls rule a kingdom of men without a complete grasp of the ways of men? How could they be queens to kings if they knew nothing about kings?

As their father unpacked the secrets of men to the young girls, the light of understanding turned on. Their eyes developed a brilliance of awareness. The girls began to understand scenarios regarding men and became less credulous. The young rulers started approaching their interactions with men from a cerebral posture. No longer were they helpless maidens. They were becoming conscious queens.

From the very beginning of time, men and women have been inseparably linked. God made Adam and Eve to co-dominate. Their productivity and fruitfulness demanded that they connect to maximize their effort. From the outset, God commanded the blessing of dominion upon mankind, inclusive of male *and* female.

For instance, Genesis 1:26 says, *And God said, Let us make man in our image, after our likeness: and let them have dominion . . .*

It says "let *them* dominate," not just *him.*

Though the man and the woman are created as partners in dominion, there are distinct roles and thinking that separates the two. Women will never get rid of men, and men certainly do not want to be exiled from women. The issue raised in this chapter deals with the necessity of the woman to understand the thinking, tendencies, and needs of men. This is not to suggest that she is a second-class citizen; rather, the reasoning behind this logic is based on the fact that men usually control society. Men are generally stronger and the aggressors of the world. Men are the terrorists of history and will abuse anything that is weak. A queen knows the male psyche and how it operates. She studies his mind so that she might protect her own position as she maintains her place of dominion in a system she did not design. A queen doesn't have to design the system to master it.

> *A woman must know the tricks of deceptive*
> *men and the needs of her God-ordained man.*

Every wise and powerful woman understands that the world is a male-dominated system. She learns the language, customs, and patterns to succeed in a system that is often established to subjugate her and her powers. She has to know that *some* men are predators seeking to devour her. She must be conscious of the tricks and schemes that will be relentlessly used against her, lest she become an unsuspecting statistic of abuse and manipulation. The Bible calls a woman who is not conscious of these things "a silly woman": *For of this sort are they which creep into houses, and lead captive silly women laden with sins, led away with divers lusts* (2 Timothy 3:6). Please don't be a silly woman.

The emphasis of this text suggests that a woman who is emotional and hormonal without being cerebral and spiritual will be used by men like a utensil. Instead, she must pay attention. I always say to my daughters that many of the men they will meet in life are prevaricating *(lying)*, perpetrating, and/or preying on clueless young women. A woman must know how men think for her own well-being, especially if she has children involved.

Would any wise woman go into a lion's cage before studying its tendencies? *No way!*

The reality for every female is that the world is a sexual and emotional hunting field—the man has the gun and the woman is the unsuspecting prey. Powerful women attempt to understand the way men think, the moves they make, and the tricks they play. She learns to discern between good and bad men, safe and dangerous men.

She may gather this insight largely from a few men who will love her unconditionally and share the pitfalls of navigating male-female relations. A simple conversation with the men in her life may save her a lifetime of pain and embarrassment. A woman might be amazed at the wisdom her dad can share if she listened. If she is really wise, she could discern that her brothers, male friends, cousins, co-workers, and father are not trying to run her life, but they are actually protecting her from imminent heart break. Men know men!

If the woman doesn't have the benefit of strong male relationships, she should recall all of her past relational experiences and connect the related, consistent traits.

A woman shouldn't simply go through relational disappointment, she should grow through it. In every heartbreak or deception are extremely valuable lessons about men. Many women choose to stay in the emotion of the pain and never come into a conscious place to revisit the experience for lessons and clues. Other women are so motivated to have another man that not only do they not learn from their past, they continue to choose the same kind of man for a lifetime.

When a woman stops and just thinks about what she's gone through, it will prove to be a world-class education in the ways of men.

A queen studies the intent of men rather than falling for his words or actions. She seeks to get to the heart of his motives and desires. She's not taken in by flattery and cheap gifts. Sometimes cheap gifts have an extremely high dollar value. It may even be a flawless diamond, but it pales in comparison to the value of the woman's soul and body which are at stake if she is taken in by a deceiver.

A queen learns the language of a man— she can hear what he's not saying.

A man may say the exact words a woman says but mean something totally different. For instance, in the act of sex the woman may say, "I love you." She means, *I am all in. I am committed completely and I'm ready to be your wife for life.* But the man may say, "I love you" and mean, *I love the sex and I don't want to close this sexual door, so I will tell you what you want to hear."* The tragedy is that he will tell this lie repeatedly and consistently as he consumes many years of the woman's life without ever making a commitment.

A woman's greatest assets to get to know men are her ears and brain. She should listen to his conversation and be honest about what she heard. Most women want the affirmation of a man so badly they lie to themselves about his true character. They foolishly believe they can change him and make him the perfect one to love them.

Women tend to close their ears and shut down their brains when it comes to romantic matters. It's always easy to identify a woman who has closed her ears and shut down her brain because she talks too much. She doesn't allow the man to disclose any information about himself while she unwisely tells him all he needs to know to manipulate her. Queens know when to shut up!

As Proverbs 29:11 says, *A fool uttereth all his mind: but a wise man keepeth it in till afterwards.* Wise women don't talk too freely with a man until they know him.

> *A queen understands her vulnerabilities.*
> *She acknowledges her female proclivity to*
> *gravitate to the appealing words of a man.*

A powerful woman realizes that predatory men will use words to circumvent her defenses. She is wise enough to understand that the right words at the right time may render her cognitively impotent; therefore, she shuts her mouth and opens her ears that she might discern the true essence of the man. The queen seeks to unveil his mind. The reason certain men won't talk is because they don't want their inner thoughts to be revealed. A powerful woman will not move forward with a man she has not studied from the inside out. Her relational advancement is in stages—a queen is never swept off her feet. Instead she vets (examines or proves) the individual campaigning for her attention. With men, the queen listens more than she speaks.

> *You cannot study a person's mind if you're speaking yours constantly. Shut up and listen!*

The same woman that will tell her toddler "Don't talk to strangers" will go to a night club and share all of her personal feelings and information with a man she has just met. Even the baby is smart enough to just look at the stranger and stare until she gets to know him.

> *How may a woman get to know a man?*
> *A queen uses dating for data.*

Don't waste the great opportunity to subtly interrogate a man when you're on a date with him by giggling and batting your eyes. The day of the dumb blonde is over. The purpose of the date should not be to explore the sexual attraction and chemistry that initially caught your attention. You need to uncover the character of the brother with wise and intentional maneuvers. You should be as meek as a lamb and as calculating as a serpent. Steve Harvey put it this way, "*Act like a woman, but think like a man.*"

You could ask questions like, "Where do you work?"

and "How long have you been there?" These questions will give you some sense of the man's stability. A man that does not have a solid work history is often a poor candidate for a serious relationship.

Another question could be, "Do you have any kids?" This opens the conversation up to indirectly acquire information regarding his enthusiasm and responsibility regarding parenting. No wise woman should entertain a man who wouldn't be a potentially good parent. Why make babies with a man who is too immature to be a father?

> *A man who is a responsible parent will take any opportunity to talk extensively about his children. If he's a deadbeat, he may be very brief in his comments.*

Another issue that may be uncovered when asking the man about his children is his relational history. A wise but stealthy line of dialogue will surely stir the man to discuss the mother or mothers of his children either negatively or affirmatively. The discerning woman may learn much about the man's character as he speaks from the truth of his emotions. She can learn whether he is a spiteful man, selfish, or disrespectful of women by how he describes the mother or mothers of his children.

A very serious question that should be asked by the Christian woman is, "Do you go to church?" His response to this question can truly give the young woman a great deal of data from which she may make some decisions. If he is blatantly anti-church, Bible, and God, there shouldn't be anything left to discuss. A man who won't follow spiritual leadership is ill-equipped to lead a wife and family in the ways of God.

*Why would a Christian woman make
herself accountable to someone who
is not accountable to anyone?*

I love the wisdom of the scripture which states in 2 Corinthians 6:14, *Be ye not unequally yoked together with
unbelievers.* An unequal yoking is a pairing that is painful and unproductive. It is far better to determine you are
incompatible early on than to ultimately face this truth
after you've invested yourself emotionally and physically.

**A queen never connects herself to a man who
does not model her values. Only kings can lead
queens. A queen consults with the men in her life**

This is somewhat a continuation of an earlier principle,
but there's nothing like a man to decode the rhetoric of
another man. If a woman does not have any males in her
family to serve as a sounding board, she should ask one
of her married girlfriends if she may talk to her husband
or significant other. The key is to get to the bottom line of
where the man's conversation is heading. Another male
can tell you if the brother's conversation is moving toward
the altar or simply the hotel room. A woman may think
he's in it for life when he's really just in it for the night.

The sad and dangerous tendency of women who desire
to be in love is to take massive risks without the benefit
of counsel. A woman like this wants it to be right so badly
that she does not want anyone to awaken her to the fact
that there are red flags. Proverbs 11:14 states, *Where no
counsel is, the people fall: but in the multitude of counsellors
there is safety.* Queens respect honest and sincere counsel.

Insight may also be attained by creating a safe group

of men to create hypothetical situations and listen to their responses. Men will often be honest about the games played by other men they don't know. For instance, a party where there are happy, relaxed, and engaged people may be a perfect environment to gather more wisdom than a woman can even retain just by casually throwing out harmless hypotheticals. She may do nothing more than begin to ask certain questions and create scenarios to leave with more knowledge than she could have hoped for.

> *A queen pays more attention to*
> *what a man doesn't say.*

Queens are always listening for what was not said. For instance, if a man is always asking to come to your "crib" and never asks you to come to his home, there are a few probabilities:
1. He lives with his mommy and has lied about his status.
2. He's married or engaged to another woman.
3. He has a place, but he doesn't want you to know where it is because he doesn't plan on sticking around after he sleeps with you.

Queens always discern what's not being said.

> *A man who has long-term intentions wants to*
> *assure a woman of his ability to provide and*
> *would eagerly display his housing situation.*

Another scenario would be a man who conveys a serious love for you but never asks about your child that he knows you have. If a man really loves you, his conversation will regularly include your kid. He's going to love what's most precious to you. At this point, it is also advisable to be very cautious and discerning because a man may also use your kid as a means of deceiving you with false affinity for the child.

Always listen for what's not being said. The Bible warns the believer to live consciously as opposed to being gullible, credulous, or oblivious. It says in 1 John 4:1, *Beloved, believe not every spirit, but try the spirits whether they are of God.*

The Spirit of God will always speak to your heart to give you an intuitive impulse. If you learn to pay attention to what you feel as opposed to what you see or hear, you will never go wrong.

> *The tendency to live in your feelings as opposed to living in the spirit or logic is a major disadvantage for women because a lie can often feel real.*

On the flip side of this issue are the queens who have already identified their kings (husbands), and contrary to the pessimistic popular opinion, all men are not dogs. There are men who will stand up, commit, and be great husbands and fathers. When a woman weeds through the parade of clowns and finds a real man, she has to know how to relate to him. A king who respects his wife, values her, provides for her, and protects her deserves a queen who meets his needs physically and emotionally. A man who supports her dreams and encourages her personal advancement should be honored.

> *A queen has the capacity to go into the mind*

of her king and to fulfill him on all levels.
She leaves no room for another woman
to gain access to her man's interest.

A powerful woman understands that her man has definite needs that should be met by his wife. In Proverbs 31, there is a description of a virtuous woman. She is a business woman, an employer, a mother, and even a philanthropist; but, she also meets all of her husband's needs. The Bible says that she meets his needs so completely that he has no justification to mess up: *The heart of her husband doth safely trust in her, so that he shall have no need of spoil* (Proverbs 31:11).

A queen will always cover every
base pertaining to her man.

If a woman thrives in her career at the expense of her family, she is out of balance. She may be a public success, but she will ultimately be a private failure. When she is dead and gone, her legacy may not recall how much money she made or how great her career was. But establishing a family that succeeds and endures will live on into the next generations. A woman who makes a good man and her family her priority should never be belittled. There's no shame in being a great wife and mother. In fact, you may be wife, mother, and career woman—it simply requires great balance and an understanding of what's most important.

A true king wants to help you do it
all—he wants you to maximize.

I must always pause to state the fact that this kind of deference by a queen is reserved for the man who would be her king, for the man who fulfills her in every way and supports her greatest potential. The male-female thought patterns are so very different that each must study the other to consistently fulfill the needs of the other. A man will fail miserably at being an effective husband if he does not invest himself into the study of his wife. Likewise, a woman will always fail at pleasing her man if she doesn't prioritize him.

A queen will actually study her king and often know him better than he knows himself.

My wife, Lisa, knows what I want, sometimes even before it registers in my mind. There are days I think I want something and she provides it before I can ask for it. It gets really spooky, at times.

God put the woman in the man's life to motivate and to assist him to greatness. In some cases, a man will rise or fall to the level of his wife. Powerful women uncover great men. The woman is the incubator of the man's destiny. The king cannot rise to his full potential without a powerful queen. The Bible says in Proverbs 18:22 that when a man is smart enough to recognize and honor a woman as his wife, he obtains favor from God. When God wants to do a man a favor, he gives him a woman.

God gave Eve to Adam for the express purpose of aiding his dominion.

Eve was Adam's helper. She helped him like one equal partner helps the other. The Bible says in Genesis 2:18,

And the Lord God said, It is not good that the man should be alone; I will make him an help meet for him.

Eve was given to Adam to add something he did not innately possess. He could not maximize without Eve; she had a tremendous influence over Adam. Queens always use their influence to elevate their men to greatness.

I have observed this very powerful principle when I was a child. My mother knew how to help my father be his very best. Their success was a team effort. She was his greatest cheerleader and the only person bold enough to correct him privately. She encouraged him when he felt low. Because she knew how to push him into his untapped potential, she changed the destiny of her children's children. She had a strong alpha male, but she knew exactly what to say, when to say it, and how to talk to motivate his greatness. She never disrespected him or attacked his manhood. She accentuated his strength with her wisdom and quiet strength. As a consequence, she steered her man into greatness of historical proportions. Till his last breath, he credited God and my mother for his success. Queens make kings.

> ***The idea that a queen has to castrate***
> ***a king to be powerful in her own right***
> ***is an anti-dominion concept.***

God made Adam and Eve differently, but equally powerful. The woman and her man are like a pair of shoes—they are independent, uniquely different, but destined to go together at the same time. A right or left shoe is in itself whole and powerful. It is when the two shoes come together that they accomplish the greater purpose of their union. Powerful women, like strong men, appreciate the impact of complimenting their man without feeling the need to substitute for him. She does not seek to be the man. She enjoys being the woman, yet equally powerful.

A woman's man is her greatest masterpiece. When she is confident and wise, she will mold that man into the king God always intended. She will recognize her influence and use it to promote him.

My father was one of the greatest religious leaders of his time. Even today, I walk through opened doors based on who my father was. But he may never have reached his highest heights if my mother, his queen, didn't deal with him like a powerful woman. She corrected him when others said nothing. She focused on the deficiencies that others were afraid to mention. She did all of this dirty work; but, she had such a grace and wisdom in knowing how to treat him that he received correction and guidance from her.

A queen knows how to handle her man to get the best out of him.

A woman must never allow others to give her a script on how to manage her man. She must know her own man and deal with him accordingly. When she knows how to handle her man, he will rise up to bless her. The virtuous woman of Proverbs 31 experienced the praises of her husband regarding the impact she made on his life.

HOW DOES A QUEEN INFLUENCE A KING?

Nobody can deny the fact that a woman has a massive influence over a man. The loose woman in the streets may manipulate a man to self-destruction. The stripper on the pole can dance a man out of all his earnings. Women and femininity are a heterosexual man's greatest weakness.

The female influence is best served when a
man's queen influences his greatness.

A man quite often becomes his best version while under the influence of his wife. A queen is always focused on using her influence to unveil the king in her man. There's a wisdom that the woman must employ to maintain a healthy and ongoing tension in her relationship with her man. The wise queen does not allow too much slack in the line between herself and her king.

A queen makes love to her king
(husband) intentionally.

For a man, sex is everything! Of course in the real world, sex isn't everything, but in a man's mind sex is extremely important. Sex is next to food, oxygen, and water. It's vital that a wife keep the love-life exciting, and the man has this responsibility, too. However, it's no secret that the enemy uses the man's sexual appetite to destroy his marriage, reputation, and career. How often have we seen public marriages ravaged because of infidelity? How many great politicians, athletes, and even ministers have been brought down because they couldn't seem to stay out of the wrong bed? Why did they put themselves in these predicaments? The number one reason is personal irresponsibility. There's no two ways about it—if I get caught up in an affair, I have no one to blame but myself.

After we've charged the man with being solely responsible for his infidelity, we must also consider a possible accessory to the crime. If a wife is romantically unavailable and sexually disinterested for months, she is not respon-sible for his actions, but she certainly aided the enemy in tempting her man. If a woman has a good man who respects and honors her, she should never allow him to feel sexually deprived apart from medical issues.

The Bible encourages husbands and wives to make sexual fulfillment a priority to avoid the possibility of temptation. Paul writes in 1 Corinthians 7:5,

> Abstaining from sex is permissible for a period of time if you both agree to it, and if it's for the purposes of prayer and fasting—but only for such times. Then come back together again. Satan has an ingenious way of tempting us when we least expect it (The Message).

Paul teaches the married population of the Corinthian church the importance of meeting the sexual obligations of marriage. What's interesting is that Paul was a single, abstinent man who understood the importance of a healthy sex life in marriage, and today we have married people who don't get it.

The powerful woman closes the door on sexual insufficiency in her marriage by becoming everything he ever dreamed of.

Let me be clear. It is never a woman's fault that a man cheats. In fact, a woman may do everything right and a childish man may still cheat. However, the wise woman is so intentional about pleasing her man that she never has to wonder if he cheated because she failed to cover him sexually. A queen can always walk away knowing that she did her part.

A queen gets involved in her king's vision.

All too often a man is left to feel that his wife is more interested in his paycheck than she is in him and his interests. In many instances, she has no clue what he does or even what he wants to accomplish because she has never asked. She only demonstrates an interest in his ability to provide for her and their kids. A queen always makes it a point to keep her priorities in order. She also makes her man know that he is her focus and priority, especially when he is a good man.

It is vital for a woman to get involved in her man's dreams. A man is always attracted to the woman who is interested in what he is interested in. What do you know about your man's dreams and goals? Do you know anything? If not, you might want to put this book down and have a conversation with your king.

A wife should never let another woman show more interest in her man's interests than she does. Whoever shares his interest will hold his interest.

I believe that the glue that has held Lisa and me together for all of our years together is that from the very start she showed more interest in my dreams and aspirations than any other woman I had ever known. She has worked tirelessly to help me maximize my potential. At times, it seemed like she was more invested in my dreams than I was.

A man needs a woman to give birth to his dreams.

I believe that it is spiritually necessary for the queen to invest herself into the dreams of her man because the queen is gifted with birthing potential—a man needs a woman to give birth to what's inside of him. Nothing comes to life without the womb, and the only womb a man has access to resides in a woman. Every man is attracted to the woman who will take his seed and grow his baby.

When the woman understands that the success and materialization of the man's vision resides in her taking that vision into her bosom and nurturing it, she will become more attentive and deliberate about getting involved with his goals.

> *A queen promotes a healthy self-esteem in her man.*

A man thrives on having a healthy self-esteem, which is when a man has his ego nurtured just enough to make him feel accomplished, equal to every task, and respected by those who matter. The greatest source of nourishment for a man's self-esteem is the attention of his woman. When a man has the affirmation of his woman, he believes he can literally do anything.

> *A queen knows how to feed her king's ego just enough to generate a confidence in him that equates to incalculable success.*

Her family and future may be transformed by a few per-fectly placed compliments and words of affirmation. If she constantly tells him he's Superman, he will eventu-ally learn how to fly.

> *One of a man's greatest needs is to feel admired and respected by his wife.*

Every man is waiting on a woman who knows how to awaken the king in him. When a woman speaks, she either stimulates her man to greatness or to ruin. A queen always speaks to the king in her man. He enters her presence as Clark Kent and exits as Superman. Queens are known to build their men up and to give birth to their greatness.

CHAPTER 3

QUEENS ARE FINANCIALLY SAVVY

QUEEN-CONSCIOUSNESS
(A Throne Is only as Secure as the Treasury)

King Paternam began to intensify the training of the young queens. He taught them that their station in life required them to be proficient in the details of running a kingdom. He explained to them that as monarchs they were totally responsible for the wellbeing of the realm and that ruling was bigger than giving orders. "Ruling," the king said, "involves making economic decisions." The young girls would have to understand that their financial decisions could not be based on momentary impulses, but visionary forecasts. They would have to make their financial decisions as if the future depended on it, because it did.

If they did not understand how to budget, save, invest, and grow the economy, there would eventually be no kingdom to rule. He gave each of them a hypothetical financial scenario to see how they would manage the kingdom. Each time, he would adjust their financial philosophies until they learned to balance the priorities properly, because a queen who mishandles money may squander her rule. A queen who does not master the treasury ultimately compromises her throne, and a throne is a terrible thing to waste.

Eventually, the king was pleased with their economic philosophies. He was encouraged that their priorities moved from merely shopping to saving, from extravagance to necessity. The king began to see the mindset of true queens manifesting in his little girls.

It has been said that one may determine the intelligence of a person by how they manage money. If this statement is true, how smart are you? How intelligent are most of the women you associate with? My father, Bishop Robert Blakes, Sr., always said, "A fool and money won't stay together too long." His words have proven to be very true. How many women do you know who are paid for a forty-hour work week on Friday and are totally broke by Saturday afternoon? Wow.

This is a generation of wasteful women and men. It is not uncommon to see a woman with an exclusive designer bag on her shoulder while simultaneously wallowing in a desperate financial condition from month to month. Why? A Gucci bag with nothing in it!

Many women splurge away the means
that are necessary to keep a roof over
their heads and to provide food for their
children. What is she thinking?

Society has poisoned the values of this generation. Average women today value looking good over actually being good. Some women today would rather pay to have their nails done and beg for their rent.

This is the era when women must take a very serious look at money matters. The idea that a woman will ultimately meet a man with a good job who will take care of her is rapidly becoming a daydream that will end in a nightmare.

A woman must have a mind to
master money for herself.

Today, the real queens are aggressively pursuing financial independence. It has been said, "The Golden Rule is this: she who has the gold makes the rules." Today's queen is no gold-digger. She has her own resources and needs no man to meet her needs, yet she knows how to drop back and let a king do what kings do.

Most women prepare only to be a wife and never maximize their personal earning potential.

When the idea of being a wife is delayed beyond the ideal date, the woman is left in an awkward position of vulnerability. She never planned to actually need her own money. She thought that she would always have a man to finance her lifestyle. Even though she never got married, there were always men willing to provide for her needs in return for romantic concessions.

Now she's older, uneducated, no career, and no work ethic of her own. What does she do? She suffers because she has fooled herself for more than half of her life. She is a professional dependent. She is no more prepared to face life than a little school girl. It's a very sad reality.

Society does not treat a woman well who cannot provide her own means. She will be stretched to limits she never imagined.

There's one thing that I am extremely proud of when it comes to my three biological daughters, Vernitra, Angel, and Rachel—they are financially independent women. The only man they have ever depended on was me, their father. I raised them to understand that the world takes advantage of women who need men to meet their needs. This is no feminist rant implying that a woman does not need a man. *Never!* I am just encouraging women to put themselves in a financial position that will provide for them if they never attain the dream wedding and marriage.

One of the things that attracted me to my wife, besides her exquisite beauty and mesmerizing eyes, was the fact that she was a working woman who was independent of my resources, though my resources were meager at that time. Do not laugh! My wife worked like a woman with a house filled with children, when the reality was that she was a single woman with no kids. She also furthered her education to qualify herself to be in position for advancement. Till this very day, my wife can survive without me and I wouldn't want it any other way. My wife has always kept good credit and saved a dollar or two or three. When we got married, she never had an eye for designer labels or fancy cars or expensive jewels. I bought her a lot of those things because it was what I wanted to see her with. She valued knowing that we had resources to meet any unexpected challenge and the money to keep our credit good. She actually improved my thinking in the area of finances.

> *A queen is financially sophisticated. She*
> *values having money over spending it*

If you are a woman who can't wait to get paid because you want to rush to the mall, you are a mentally-weak woman without vision. *Don't shoot the messenger!* The Bible says in Proverbs 21:20: *There is treasure to be desired and oil in the dwelling of the wise; but the foolish man spendeth it up.*

If you have more money on your person than you have in your bank accounts, you are a clueless woman who is probably suffering from low self-esteem. *Once you really*

*know who you are, you will no longer live to impress the
world with a façade of prosperity.* You will use your means
to provide for one of your greatest needs, which is security.

A queen values financial security
over all other things.

Queens value having money because at all times they
need to know the kingdom (family) is secure. Next to God,
money is a sense of security. As wise old Solomon put it in
Ecclesiastes 7:12: *For wisdom is a defense, and money is a
defense.* Money defends the family against incidents, acci-
dents, and predicaments. Queens value money!

Money is designed to provide protection from hard-
ship and calamity. The woman must respect every dime
because God meant it to be a means of security. Sometimes the woman cannot rely on another to provide her
security, so she must take it into her own hands.

When the woman disrespects
money, it exits her life.

Anything that we disrespect will avoid our presence. Powerful women have a healthy relationship with making
money, managing money, and multiplying money. As a
consequence, they magnetize and master money.

There are two specific women in the Bible which I
would like for us to examine. Each of them teaches us
something powerful about women and money. Both of
these women were married, and yet at some point they
took control of their financial future.

*Even married women should assert
themselves financially.*

A married woman does not have the luxury of being financially illiterate or economically oblivious. She cannot afford
to do this because her children's future is at stake. Her ability to grow old and secure is on the line. A woman should
not sit and hope that all is well. Queens always know the
state of the kingdom's economy.

*A true king wants his queen to be as financially
independent as possible because at any moment
the entire realm could be in her control.*

A TALE OF TWO WOMEN

The Poor, Widowed Woman
The first of the two biblical women we will observe is a
woman who was married to a good and godly man. He was
a preacher and was apparently in good standing with spiritual leadership; however, he died and he left his family in
a very precarious financial predicament. A person may love
God and practice all of the spiritual principles of tithing,
sowing seed, and whatever else, but if there is no financial discipline, it usually ends in financial catastrophe. Even
though he loved God, he still died in debt.

*The spiritual principles must always be
reinforced by the practical principles
of money management.*

Let's take a look at the biblical account of this widowed woman in 2 Kings 4:1-7:

> *Now there cried a certain woman of the wives of the sons of the prophets unto Elisha, saying, Thy servant my husband is dead; and thou knowest thay thy servant did fear the LORD: and the creditor is come to take unto him my two sons to be bondmen.*
>
> *And Elisha said unto her, What shall I do for thee? Tell me, what hast thou in the house? And she said, Thine handmaid hath not any thing in the house, save a pot of oil.*
>
> *Then he said, Go, borrow thee vessels abroad of all thy neighbours, even empty vessels; borrow not a few.*
>
> *And when thou art come in, thou shalt shut the door upon thee and upon thy sons, and shalt pour out into all those vessels, and thou shalt set aside that which is full.*
>
> *So she went from him, and shut the door upon her and upon her sons, who brought the vessels to her; and she poured out.*
>
> *And it came to pass, when the vessels were full, that she said unto her son, Bring me yet a vessel. And he said unto her, There is not a vessel more. And the oil stayed.*
>
> *Then she came and told the man of God. And he*

said, Go, sell the oil, and pay thy debt, and live
thou and thy children of the rest.

This woman was thrown into a very difficult financial dilemma because of the death of her husband. He died prematurely and he left his family in debt. As a consequence, the creditors came to enslave his sons to pay off his debts. *The harsh reality about financial irresponsibility is that the next generation will often pay for it.* This man possibly made some poor financial choices and his family was left to struggle with the consequences.

A queen gets involved in the financial matters of the family.

A woman inserting herself into the financial picture is not challenging her husband's authority or leadership. A woman needs to be privy to what is going on financially because the well-being of her and her children is often hanging in the balance. It is a wise woman who makes sure that her family is financially sound. It is a weak man who is not comfortable with empowering his wife to function intelligently within the financial system of the family.

The woman of Proverbs 31 knew that all was well in her household. In Proverbs 31:27, it says, *She looketh well to the ways of her household.* If you have no clue about the financial status of your family, you are not looking well to the ways of your house.

As a wife, you owe it to your husband and children to take a more assertive role in the financial picture of your family. What happens if he is incapacitated? How can you take care of him and them if you are financially illiterate and ignorant of your own finances? You don't want to be in a position where you are blindsided because of ignorance.

As a husband and father, my primary goal is to protect my family. If I am not present, I certainly don't want money to be an issue. I applaud my wife for being strong enough to make certain that she exercises foresight and secures her future with or without me. The wife of 2 Kings 4 would have done well if she had done her due diligence while her husband lived. What if she had asked questions and had inserted herself into the financial picture sooner? What if he had enjoyed the benefit of her ideas? They might have gotten through their financial challenge together. Who knows, it may have been financial stress that killed him. His wife may have been able to save his life.

There are a few facts that we pull from the experience of this widowed woman. *We may deduce that she was ignorant of the financial status of her family because she did not get alarmed until her sons were threatened with slavery.* The image is that she was unpleasantly surprised.

Queens never leave themselves in a position of ignorance pertaining to life-and-death matters.

TIMELESS TREASURY TIPS FOR EVERY QUEEN

1. A Queen Always Knows Her Financial Reality.
The widowed woman of 2 Kings 4 couldn't do anything about her situation until she got the facts. As long as she was in the dark, her ignorance kept her beneath the circumstances. Things did not change until she knew the hard truth.

Facing your financial facts can be a bone-chilling experience, but a true queen realizes she must know for the sake of those depending on her.

The interesting truth is that either you go and search for the financial facts of your life, or they will one day find you, as they did this lady. A wise and competent woman does not avoid the inconvenient truth—she will face the facts either sooner or later. The sooner you get the facts, the better are the chances that you can make a favorable outcome.

For instance, there are many people who have no clue what their debt-to-income ratio, credit rating, or budget should be. This is because they simply don't want to face their financial truth. To be financially strong and secure is to keep your eyes on your business and to know what is going on, even when the picture is not presently pretty.

2. A Queen Only Gets Counsel from Proven Financial Sources.

After the widow woman of the text learns of the situation, she immediately seeks the counsel of the Prophet Elisha. It's interesting that she didn't find a close friend. This is significant because usually the people who are in our circle share our circumstances. She was wise enough to know that a part of their financial solution was to actually receive counsel from someone who was not in the same boat.

Sometimes you have to step outside of your circle to change your circumstances.

The mistake that many people make is to get counsel from those who are as limited as they are. People who share poverty often also share advice. If you want to change your financial condition, you must talk to someone who is on another level financially.

I love the way Proverbs 28:11 puts it: *The rich man is wise in his own conceit; but the poor that hath understanding searcheth him out.* A queen will find financial mentors to follow in her quest for economic elevation and dominion.

3. A Queen Respects Her Present Resources.

The counsel that the prophet gave to the widowed woman made her think about what she already possessed—he counseled her to take inventory of her present resources. What she needed to get to where she wanted to go was already in her possession. She had a little pot of oil and it was that very oil that was the seed to her financial freedom.

> *A queen's financial increase always starts with respecting the little money she currently has.*

In a parable found in Matthew 25:21, Jesus says: *His lord said unto him, Well done, thou good and faithful servant: thou hast been faithful over a few things, I will make thee ruler over many things.*

Respect for what you now possess is the starting point of abundance. If you won't do the right thing with a small paycheck, you shouldn't expect limitless means. Every million dollars begins with holding on to the first penny. A queen is aware that it is not how much a person makes, it is how much she keeps. Every dime leads to a dollar, and dollars turn into fortunes.

The woman who squanders small sums eventually drains her future.

The widowed woman of 2 Kings 4 followed the instruction of the prophet and took control of the little oil she possessed, and it multiplied. It grew beyond her capacity to imagine.

The supernatural power of God won't move beyond your personal financial disciplines.

4. A Queen Pays Her Debts.

The end of the story is that her means increased super-naturally. After her increase, Elisha instructed her to make her husband's name good before she did anything else. He told her to pay off her husband's debts. When the prophet instructs her to pay the debts, this was the equivalent of teaching her to make good credit a priority. When you pay your bills, you are building a financial profile that will afford you respect in high places.

Average women quite often ruin their reputation by failing to pay what is owed. The result is unbelievably low credit ratings. Then when it is time to buy a car, she may not be financed or she will only get a godless rate. When it is time to purchase a home, she won't be qualified because she failed to pay for a designer bag or some other out-standing, often unnecessary, unpaid debt which destroys her financial profile.

A queen has good credit.

When a woman pays her debts, she may acquire other people's resources to build her future. Good credit is equivalent to having a good name, which will cause other people to lend you their resources for your plans. With these resources, you may strategically expand your borders and territory.

When a woman has good credit, she gets the cheap-est interest rates. Banking institutions will provide her with lines of credit to make financial moves. If her credit is good enough, she may be favored to purchase valuable assets, like real estate, without anything down. Her very signature can bring great wealth when her name is good.

The Bible says in Proverbs 22:1, *A good name is rather*

to be chosen than great riches, and loving favour rather than silver and gold.

I vividly remember when I was in Chicago, Illinois for a "Father Daughter Talk" meeting and I was teaching about the importance of a woman and her credit. I was saying that a woman should have at least a 750 score. To my amazement there was a young black sister who raised her voice and said, "I have a score over 800." I was impressed to see a single black woman with a score so high. This is the kind of consciousness and stewardship queens must possess today.

A TALE OF TWO WOMEN

The Wealthy, Virtuous Woman

In contrast to the widowed woman of 2 Kings 4, there is another biblical example of a powerful woman who had an excellent perspective and set a tremendous example for all women. She is the virtuous woman of Proverbs 31. She was the wife of a powerful leader in the community. She was well provided for, and yet she established a standard of economic consciousness that every queen should follow. She had her own businesses and enterprises despite having a plush domestic situation. She applied herself relative to personal earning. She did not take having a strong financial provider for a husband as an opportunity to be financially indifferent. I encourage you to read the whole account of the virtuous woman; it will bless you.

Proverbs 31:16 says: *She considereth a field, and buyeth it: with the fruit of her hands she planteth a vineyard.* We see her making big moves, even as a married woman.

*A wise woman prepares to handle business
even in the best of circumstances, because
she never knows what the future holds.*

HOW DOES A WOMAN ACCOMPLISH
FINANCIAL DOMINANCE?

1. A Queen Educates Herself.

This is the wrong time to be an ignorant woman. A woman today must take advantage of every educational opportunity. Formal education is preferable, but taking the personal initiative to read and study can place a woman in an advantageous position. Knowledge equates into dollars—the world respects smart women.

*High heels and a low IQ is usually
fashionable poverty.*

I have the greatest respect for my mother, Lois Blakes. My mom was a wife and mother who chose to finish her undergraduate and graduate degrees. My mother chose to be as smart as she was beautiful.

2. A Queen Goes to Work.

The virtuous woman was wealthy and working. A woman must always think about working today. Sitting on your bottom and waiting for a man to finance your survival as a single woman cannot be an option. A powerful woman will always have her own means. When you have to depend on another for your needs, you subconsciously become a mental slave.

As the Bible puts it, *The rich ruleth over the poor, and the borrower is servant to the lender* (Proverbs 22:7).

A single woman should make employment her greatest ambition. She should never put her head on the pillow at the mercy of any man or government for her sustenance.

> *Even in the case of a woman who has a hard-working man, the cost of living often demands multiple incomes.*

A woman should have the mind to work at any time. Things are so unpredictable and the global economy can be so volatile that two incomes is more frequently a necessity. This is the age of the "Power Couple."

3. A Queen Expands Her Financial Literacy.

A queen learns all of the terminology relative to investing, trading, and money matters. She gets a comprehensive understanding of how to make money grow and how to move it around. The woman of Proverbs 31 understood the language of money.

June Collier, a financial adviser, explains in his video on why the wealthy don't use banks—that the most a bank will pay on money in one of their common cash equivalent accounts (certificates of deposit, checking, savings, money markets, savings bonds, and treasury bills) is 0.15%. The same bank will then loan you money and charge you 10.99% on the low end and to 22.99% on the high end.[1] These numbers are from 2015. The bank takes the money you deposit and they invest it at higher rates of return, pay

---

1   https://www.youtube.com/watch?v=vsRkzbtQf_g

you nothing, and rob you when you borrow the money you made for them through your deposits.

*A queen learns the financial
game and plays it well.*

Banks can be used as a holding place until you discover where your money should be invested, and that's it. Even in Matthew 25:26-27, Jesus talks about a master who left certain assets with his servants. Two of them increase what he had given them, but one simply hides what was given to him in the earth—he doesn't increase it at all. When the master returns and finds that he did nothing to grow his allotment, he calls the servant "wicked" and says, "The least you could have done would have been to bring my money to the banker that I might get a little interest." Queens always understand that the bank is the least they may do with money. Queens investigate things like real estate, precious metals, and stocks to wisely invest in.

4. A Queen Lives Below Her Means.
A queen never lives at or above her means. She never does all that she can do. Her wisdom says to put something away for a leaner day. She is never caught with an empty store because she always monitors her spending habits.

The Bible says in Proverbs 21:20, *There is treasure to be desired and oil in the dwelling of the wise; but a foolish man spendeth it up.*

A queen never spends it all!

CHAPTER 4

QUEENS MAXIMIZE THEIR POTENTIAL

QUEEN-CONSCIOUSNESS
(A Queen Is Only Limited by Her
Perception and Ambition)

Just as King Paternam felt like he was making great progress with the young princesses, he was taken aback. In a very relaxed and casual moment, he asked his daughters about their ambitions in life. He expected to hear them say that they would rule and reign, marry great kings, and expand the empire to the four corners of the world.

Instead, he was heartbroken to hear shallow and average responses. These were daughters of a king! They could go and do anything in the world, but their ambitions barely got them past the courtyard of the palace. The king realized that they were still detoxing from the low self-esteem they were indoctrinated with in his absence.

The king began to share with them their great heritage. He explained to them that they had royal blood and that the entire kingdom was theirs. He encouraged them to shoot for the moon because they would surely attain to it. With tears in his eyes, he begged them to always reach for their dreams in every situation. The girls gathered around their loving father and promised they would. Something shifted in their souls when their father told them who they were and challenged them to be their best.

Let's get this clear immediately—you cannot maximize your life without a very constant and sure relationship with God. You may apply all of these principles and yet still be far beneath your potential or purpose. The reason you must start with God is because He is the only one who can give you your purpose and empower you to reach it. The Bible says in Proverbs 31:30 that *a woman that feareth the Lord, she shall be praised.*

A queen's quest is always for self-actualization. She has so much potential, the challenge is to find ways to fulfill it. Queens are so engaged in self-fulfillment they are rarely distracted with the concerns of others.

> ***A queen is on a quest for self-discovery and doesn't have time to waste on pointless endeavors.***

A common mark of women who have been psychologically marginalized by social pressures is that they tend to live in a perpetual state of mediocrity. They settle for manifesting less than 100% of their true potential. Society says, "Just settle for looking good and don't worry about such lofty personal goals as education, equality, and financial freedom." Average women yield to these external constricting influences and usually die with their tank of potential still full because they fail to maximize or use it.

> ***Average women will value less important items than their own personal growth.***

For instance, many women will ignore their true vision to make a less ambitious man comfortable. I've had women with great credit and making enough money to afford their own homes choose to stay in a lower position to keep an inferior man appeased. More times than I'd like to acknowledge, they opt out of home ownership because they think it might turn him off. They don't want to appear too accomplished; it might intimidate the men. So, they settled for mediocrity. Other women buy in to social trends just to fit into some certain group, even when the trend works against their personal value systems and principles.

> *Weak women are "group thinkers"—*
> *they run with the pack. A queen is*
> *most comfortable standing alone.*

The clearest mark of a real queen is that she always strives to be her best and most authentic self. She realizes that the Creator has designed her with specific gifts, talents, and abilities that must be manifested. She lives her life to glorify God and to edify others. Jesus called this way of living *fruitfulness*.

In John 15:8; he said, *Herein is my Father glorified, that ye bear much fruit; so shall ye be my disciples*. Every well-adjusted individual lives to bear the fruit the Creator programmed her for. Self-actualization is simply the process of a woman giving birth to everything that God put within her, living a fruitful life based on God's original design and intent for her.

I have three biological daughters and each of them is unique: One is an educator, one a business woman, and the other an aspiring actress and psychologist. Each of them has followed her unique purpose, and we have encouraged the young queens to self-actualize. I've taught them to never be intimidated by another person, but rather to compete with the vision that is within their own hearts.

The Creator has put an image of the best version of you within you. Do not allow society, people, or religion to rob you of yourself.

A QUEEN'S POTENTIAL DEVELOPS LIKE A SEED

A good example of self-actualization is found in a seed. Every seed is created with a particular DNA and ideally it should produce the fruit it was created to manifest, providing it is in the right conditions. You never see an apple seed producing a lemon. If you plant an orange seed and it actually brings forth a pear, you should call CNN immediately because it would be an agricultural miracle. *If nature understands that it must actualize according to the Creator's plan, why do women not focus on the Creator's intentions for them?*

In the case of women, most produce everything but the genius God intended. How often have we seen young women who had presidential potential succumb to the pressures of society and end up with multiple pregnancies, in poverty, and uneducated? How did she miss her greatness? What robbed her of the total manifestation of her royalty? How does a queen end up begging?

We may look at the germination process of the seed and glean some very specific principles for the woman's self-actualization. The seed goes through a particular evolution that may be likened to the process every woman can embrace if she will manifest her untapped potential.

1. The Seed Comes from the Core.
The seed is the incubator of potential—it is the pod of destiny. The only way to get to the seed is to cut to the core of a fruit. The potential is within. I heard Bishop T.D. Jakes

expound on this process, saying in essence: *"You can plant the skin of a fruit or the meat of it and never get reproduction. The only way to reproduce the fruit is to get to the seed of the fruit."* When I heard this I was blown away. I thought about the years I'd wasted on shallow ambitions or surface priorities when my greatness was always at my core. How many women have I known who believe the idea that their greatest contribution is what they may present to the world on the outside? They actually believe that their size, looks, and fashion are the greatest assets of their person. They are caught up in the aspects that will never reproduce the Creator's greatness programmed within.

On a deeper level, women are being socially conditioned to search for their total identity in the shallow surface levels of their external lives. Women are being driven to beauty and sex as opposed to understanding that their power is internal. It's not the wrapping, it's the content.

Every conscious queen is in touch with her core.

A queen is strong and healthy from within. Common women never maximize because they live on the surface and never journey to the deeper recesses of their inner being. Do not focus on the packaging instead of the content because the value is always on the inside, not the outside.

The word of God speaks frequently of the importance of the heart and its impact on our self-actualization. Proverbs 4:23 states: *Keep thy heart with all diligence; for out of it are the issues of life.*

The heart in this context speaks of the inner being—the soul and spirit regions. It is the intangible aspects of the person. The heart is a place that is not easily accessed. It requires effort and intent for the woman to live from her heart; but, the heart is where the true potential resides. If the woman is to actualize, she must get to her core. Things like meditation, vision mapping, and prayer are some exercises that aim at the core. Education and worship are also core disciplines. When the woman is done shopping, she should have a book on her nightstand, be enrolled in a class or two, and be in hot pursuit of God.

A woman's self-actualization demands that she trim away all of the superficial elements and go directly to her core, which is her spirit.

2. The Seed Has to be Planted.

Once the seed is attained, it is then planted into the soil. This planting almost feels like a waste of potential—to take a perfectly good seed and just bury it in dirt. As it relates to the woman's actualization or the fulfilling of her potential, this action represents the process of self-denial which always precedes self-actualization. The wisdom of the scriptures suggests that she must lose herself to find herself. Many sisters never manifest their greatness because they never invest themselves into the soils of humility or service to others. It is only under the cover of selfless intent that the seed of her potential may germinate. Today, sisters have taken a "diva's" approach to living which has shifted many from the base of servanthood. Servanthood is the prerequisite for reigning.

You will only discover your best version as you are firmly planted in service to others.

I love the way Jesus Christ himself put it in Matthew 16:25, *For whosoever will save his life shall lose it: and whosoever will lose his life for my sake shall find it.* Jesus says when you sow your life into the things that matter to God and benefit humanity, you will find your life. When you attempt to preserve your life for your own selfish agenda, you will ultimately waste your life.

> *The true queen understands that her self-manifestation is in serving and giving herself to things which are selfless.*

As prominent as the biblical woman of Proverbs 31 was, she lived a life that was of service to others. She was wealthy and powerful, but her life was based in service. She served her husband and kids as well as the poor.

> *Real queens serve.*

When the woman makes an investment of herself into something that is selfless and separate from personal ambitions, she allows her spirit to open up. *The spirit is God's production center of all greatness. God has designed us so that a woman must give herself to find herself.*

Now, let's return to our analogy of the seed and how it relates to realizing one's full potential. In the case of the seed, it gets all of the nutrients it needs from the very soil it's buried in. The seed is getting precisely what it needs there. While it seems to be compromised because of its position, it is actually exactly where it needs to be to manifest its greatness.

A queen is not nourished by the high places in
life, she is nourished by the lowest places.

The award ceremonies and six-figure incomes are not the things that bring value to your life. Value, power, and meaning come from the times you lift others. You are empowered when you are empowering the powerless. A queen finds her strength in using her power for those who have none. She gets nothing out of walking above people; instead, she finds life in reaching down and making herself to appear less than all.

3. The Seed Must Be Watered.
The third phase of the seed's development is that it must be watered. The water causes the seed to germinate as it lies buried. The water facilitates a connection between the seed and the soil.

The water ignites the life that is contained
in the seed.

To be watered speaks of being refreshed and supplied with an essential for life. If the seed does not live, it will never produce fruit. It can only live where it may be watered. *This is symbolic of the woman who must have certain support systems in place to empower her potential.*

A queen must intentionally place
herself in environments that support
and nurture her greatness.

A queen should never plant herself where she is not watered. A powerful woman will release friends and separate from men who don't bring out her best. She will never invest herself in a place that does not empower her. She has no time to waste.

To live in a queen's state of mind is to live with no tolerance for pointless relationships or futile endeavors.

> *To self-actualize will demand that the queen stay close to people who inspire her development.*

When a woman has the right relationships, those connections feed into her development. A queen chooses relationships on purpose. Relationships must fuel her development and her rule. As a queen you must never engage in relationships that diminish you. You should not have to compromise your goals and vision to accommodate a person of lesser capacity. You must never maintain friendships or love affairs that drain your enthusiasm.

As a spiritual father and mentor to thousands of women across the nation, the one thing I struggle with is getting these queens to understand the importance of developing and maintaining relationships that support their future.

A relationship that works for where you are now is not necessarily going to be conducive for your future. Every woman should ask herself, *"Will this relationship support the weight of my manifested potential?"*

> *Many relationships have expiration dates that should not be ignored.*

4. The Seed Reaches for the Sun.
When the seed is planted firmly and watered sufficiently, the only thing left to do is reach for the sun.

The seed naturally grows in the
direction of its highest perspective.

The seed initially feels the pull of the sun as it grows under the cover of the soil it's planted in. It is not long before the seed produces a sprout. Once that sprout is visible, it is focused on nothing but the sun. *Powerful women always set their sights on points that transcend their immediate circumstances.* A queen is never focused on things surrounding her, she is focused on things above and transcending.

A queen is so focused on where she is going,
she never gets bogged down in where she is.

Broken love affairs will not stagnate a powerful woman, because she is focused on something higher. The betrayal of false friends will never depress her to the point she gives up on life, because she sees her future. A queen always reaches for higher heights. Temporary financial challenges won't break her, for she knows where she's going.

Queens keep their highest aspirations in view. They don't get distracted by side issues; rather, their focus is locked in on the highest point.

I love the way *The Message* characterizes the virtuous woman of Proverbs 31. In verses 17-18, it states, *First thing in the morning, she dresses for work, rolls up her sleeves, eager to get started. She senses the worth of her work, is in no hurry to call it quits for the day.*

This Proverbs woman was clearly focused and reaching for her specific goals with every moment of her time and ounce of her energy. This was a queen on a mission who could not be distracted. ✳ ✳ ✳

*Every time you've been distracted, it was
because you took your eyes off the goal.*

ADVANTAGES OF A SELF-ACTUALIZED WOMAN

There are remarkable benefits that come alongside of a woman who actualizes her true power. Women who know who they are and are unapologetic about it walk with a distinct sense of control and grace.

*When you actually step completely into
your potential, it is going to introduce you
to a life you didn't know was possible.*

1. A Self-Actualized Woman Is More Easily Identified by Her Husband.
The common error made by single women who are hoping for a good mate is to become so consumed with looking for a man that they lose themselves. The surest way to be positioned for recognition by the right man is to be fully invested in your own development.

*It takes a whole and healthy woman to
attract a whole and healthy man.*

Too often, women want kings before they have become queens. If you want a man who will know who he is and possess the capacity to appreciate and love you properly, *you must know who you are and be fully invested into the development of yourself.*

Women who are consumed with manifesting
their potential are identified by husbands
easier, happy by themselves, and eventually
make great mates for great men.

There are a few biblical women who demonstrate how a self-actualized woman is attractive to a quality man. There was a woman by the name of Ruth who attracted the attention of a wealthy man named Boaz. He was intrigued by how she was ignoring him and taking care of her own business. *When a woman focuses on being her best self, she will consistently attract men of superior character.*

Another example is seen in the account of how Abraham's servant went to search for a wife for the young prince Isaac in Genesis 24:17-24. The servant identified her as he watched her go about her business, unaware that she was under observation or examination.

The clearest evidence of a woman who is
fully invested in her personal development
is that she is happy in her current state.

A woman with a queen's state of mind does not need to add anything to her life to feel happy. She is content as she is. She is never depressed because she may be thirty years old and unmarried, or she hasn't had a kid yet. She stays in the moment and is grateful for every day.

2. A Self-Actualized Woman Lives with a Sense of Fulfillment.

There is no substitute for personal fulfillment. A woman may have all of the money in the world, the man of any woman's dreams, and fame to match, but if she puts her head on her pillow at night and does not feel a sense of personal fulfillment she will not be happy.

> *God has so designed the system so that fulfillment, which leads to happiness, never comes from anything outside of you.*

A queen understands that she will only find fulfillment within herself and God. She knows that a relationship will not fulfill her. She's aware that a baby will not bring fulfillment. Fulfillment must come from within the core of herself.

> *The only means of fulfillment is to do the very thing that God placed you on the planet to do.*

I had a conversation with one of my spiritual daughters one evening after Bible study. She explained to me that she was running from the call of God on her life. So, I shared some wisdom with her. I informed her that she would never really find happiness until she submitted to the will of God for her life. I also told her that everything she was reaching for as she attempted to escape God's call would be abundantly provided when she submitted to Him. My message was clear—if you want to be happy and fulfilled, surrender to God and His purpose for your life.

> *When a woman seeks, finds, and functions in God's purpose for her life, she lives with a true sense of peace and power.*

Isaiah 26:3 puts it in very plain terms: *Thou wilt keep him in perfect peace, whose mind is stayed on thee: because he trusteth in thee.* The wisdom of this ancient text is this: when God and His purposes are your priority, you have everything that matters.

Never get your priorities mixed up. First things must always come first, and the first thing a queen must put on her agenda is personal wellbeing. That statement may sound self-serving, but the reality is that you cannot be of service to anyone else if you are not whole and happy. Even the Bible tells us that we should love others as we love ourselves (Matthew 22:39).

Sometimes the best thing a wife and mother may do for her family is to focus on her own wellbeing. When she is fulfilled, she is empowered to minister to them.

3. A Self-Actualized Woman Destroys Generational Curses.
When a woman self-actualizes, or reaches her full potential as a queen, she breaks the shackles of social conditioning that destroy the vision and diminish the ambition of generations of young women.

Women need to see other women who beat the odds.

When the world looks at an Oprah Winfrey, it resets the possibility meter in the minds of millions of women. When African American women saw Michelle Obama stand next to her husband as he was sworn in as the president of the United States of America, it made women of color all over the world take a new and more favorable look at themselves. When Hillary Clinton won the popular vote for president over Donald Trump by nearly three-million votes, the psychological barriers were shattered for young queens worldwide.

> *When a woman maximizes her life, she transforms the lives of all women who are looking on.*

You need to manifest your true potential because your daughters, nieces, and neighbors are being energized by your growth. Queen Esther risked her life to manifest her God-ordained purpose, but she consciously did it for the salvation of others.

HOW DOES A QUEEN SELF-ACTUALIZE?

1. A Queen Self-Actualizes When She Uses Her Gifts in the Area of Her Passion.
There is such a thing as being a successful failure. A successful failure is one that is accomplished in something God never created them to do. We often get achievement confused with success and fulfillment. There are many women who have achieved unbelievable success, but they are unfulfilled and are still a failure because they have yet to manifest their inner self.

> *Self-actualization always starts with knowing your gifts and using your gifts to satisfy the hunger of your inner passion.*

2. A Queen Self-Actualizes When She Formulates a Vision for Her Life.
A vision is simply a written declaration of where you are going and a step-by-step plan to get there. A vision is simply a destiny map.

*A queen may never actualize what
she has not clearly defined.*

Take the time today to write your vision out plainly. The word of God instructs us to write the vision. Habakkuk 2:2-3 says,

> And the Lord answered me, and said, Write the vision, and make it plain upon tables, that he may run that readeth it.

> For the vision is yet for an appointed time, but at the end it shall speak, and not lie: though it tarry, wait for it; because it will surely come, it will not tarry.

When a woman has a written vision for her life, she can easily discern who fits into her life and who doesn't. When a woman has a vision for her life, she awakens each day with purpose and energy.

**A queen with vision avoids relationships
that might divorce her from herself.**

A queen's vision defines her parameters, especially with relationships. I believe that a common tendency among women who fail to manifest and maximize their full potential is that they often waste their lives with people who strangle them spiritually, emotionally, financially, and professionally. They tend to love toxic people more than they love themselves. A relationship that divorces the woman from herself is any relationship that demands she put her values and goals in storage to accommodate the other person. It's like a person staying with you but they demand that you move your furniture out while they redecorate your house with their furniture. It's a relationship that leaves her empty and feeling guilty about things done or left undone. A relationship that divorces the woman from herself is any relationship that consumes the woman's thoughts with drama and extreme compromises that are never reciprocated. It is a relationship that constantly makes withdrawals and never deposits. It drains her while never replenishing.

The Bible puts it best in Amos 3:3: *Can two walk together, except they be agreed?* The commonsense revelation of this text is that it is impossible for one to travel north while another travels south. The best they can do is to wave at each other as they pass by one another.

A queen actualizes by never lying to herself about relationships that are not on the same page.

3. A Queen Self-Actualizes by Maintaining Mentors and Coaches in Every Vital Area of Life.

Queen Esther had mentors who helped her maximize her potential.

Her relative Mordecai was her primary mentor. She also had people who helped her through her perfecting process as she got ready to meet the king. People who self-actualize learn to connect with the people who can sharpen their disciplines in all areas. The Bible says that as iron sharpens iron, so a man sharpens another (Proverbs 27:17). Another passage that supports the necessity of mentors is seen in Proverbs 9:9 which says, *Give instruction to a wise man, and he will be wiser: teach a just man, and he will increase in learning.*

For a queen to actualize she must expand her circle

to mentors, counsellors, coaches, and advisers who can
add to her base. ☙

CHAPTER 5

QUEENS ELIMINATE INSECURITY AND NEGATIVITY

QUEEN-CONSCIOUSNESS
(Insecurity and Royalty Will Never Coexist)

As the great king Paternam continued to educate his three princesses, Honestum, Imperium, and Potestatem, he observed how they interacted with each other. He knew that their capacity to work together as a sisterhood might one day be their salvation.

The king, in a strategic maneuver, also invited refined young ladies of the court to visit the royal chambers. He wanted to observe the chemistry between the girls and those he considered to be their contemporaries. The king understood that the presence of a regal starts with self-confidence in every situation.

*King Paternam observed that the sisters worked well together; but, when he brought in the other young women they became quiet and withdrawn. Imperium started to feel angry at the other young women. The king recognized insecurity within the young queens **and he was livid!***

*When the young visitors departed the royal quarters, the king sat the girls down and explained to them that the strange and uneasy feeling they experienced when the other girls visited was **insecurity**. He explained that insecurity and royalty could never coexist. He also explained why they had no reason to ever feel insecure. They were born to rule and no one could wear their crowns. It didn't matter how talented, beautiful, or smart the others may have been...those other girls could never be them. **They were queens.***

There's little in life more unbecoming than an attractive, educated, and otherwise intelligent woman who struggles with insecurity. The entire world is often puzzled at her identity crisis and wonders how she cannot realize her true power and strength. She's actually a queen with the mentality of a slave. A slave in mind is a slave in life. It does not matter what your position is, if your disposition is something else you will always live at the level of your mindset.

Many dear, single sisters often wonder why certain brothers never make a serious advance in their direction: *Why don't they call again or attempt to develop something more than a platonic relationship?* As I have had years of experience teaching women nationally and internationally, I have been called on for advice and I've heard all of the stories. I also have the benefit of discussing these very issues with young and older men. The most common response I get from Godly and eligible men as to why they don't pursue certain women is because their insecurity and negativity is a turn off. A sister may believe she's done a good job disguising her issues, but in reality they stand out like a lighthouse lamp across a dark sea. Everybody sees it!

> *When a king comes to call for a queen, she must*
> *be a queen on all levels—mind, body, and spirit.*

Why are beautiful, educated, and godly women so insecure? Why do they feel so inferior? This sense of personal deficiency is no fault of the woman. Women have been taught to think of themselves as inferiors. The world is breeding insecure women. The world does not really like a confident woman. Just ask Shirley Chisolm, Maya Angelou, Margaret Thatcher, or Oprah Winfrey. They are all figures of strength and achievement; they are also warriors who bucked the system, as all queens must. The strong and secure women of every era have been so because they went against societal norms and refused to be programmed.

A confident woman is misunderstood and labeled as some sort of negative social cancer by the world. A confident woman is frowned upon and viewed with disdain. Society intentionally incapacitates a woman's confidence to keep her in a place of mental enslavement to a false sense of inferiority. For instance, for a woman to do the same job as a man and not be paid an equal wage is a means of institutional marginalization and psychological positioning.

All around the world, governments and the powers that be intentionally promote the things that rob the woman of her independence and personal confidence.

Think about it. The various limits that are imposed upon women through media, religion, government, and even the oral tradition of their own forefathers is usually unfounded. The main sentiment communicated is, "A woman cannot be equal to a man." What is that supposed to mean? As a man, I do believe that there are physical differences between men and women which may limit the woman in some physical acts of strength, but apart from the anatomical differences, there is nothing that a woman cannot handle. I believe that they are typically more cognitive than the man and often more spiritual. The root of the woman's inferiority is in the way she has been trained by society, what she believes as a consequence of that training and her diminished self-definition.

*The woman's inferiority is not innate, it is
introduced through an intentional system that
creates a self-contained prison of self-doubt.*

God did not make you a weak, defeated, angry, and insecure woman. This is the wrong world for a weak and scared
woman. Snap out of it! You are no one's victim. You were
designed to conquer and to be in full, confident control
of your gifts and abilities.

If you check out Eve, the first woman, she was a dom-
inator. Queen Esther was a confident and bold woman.
The judge Deborah was a mighty leader. Where did you
get this notion that you are to be a mere dependent or
victim? If you are insecure and timid, it did not come from
God. Every woman was designed to be an alpha-female.
Too few accept the challenge.

Second Timothy 1:7 puts it in the plainest language
when it says, *For God hath not given us the spirit of fear;
but of power, and of love, and of a sound mind.*

The text is very clear—God does not give us a spirit
of timidity. Rather, He gives us the spirit of power and a
strong mind.

*You are insecure because you were
trained to be. Insecurity is not a built-in
character trait, it is a conditioned behavior.
Somebody taught you to feel insecure.*

The Holy Spirit spoke to me about the insecurities of
women and how they are formed: A perverted male-dominated society trains women to think and see themselves
as inferiors. This is an intentional, satanic system of deception to break the woman's sense of dominion. The same

men that teach her to think less of herself are the very predators that plunder her power, diminish her perceived worth to her sexuality, and use her brilliance as they take the credit. Once society infiltrates the woman's thinking, she becomes a slave to the lie.

Insecurity is a mindset which leads to behaving beneath one's potential and makes one subordinate to others.

The conditioning of the woman is not unlike taming a powerful animal. The elephant always has the capacity to crush the little man with the whip. Why doesn't he? He has been sufficiently trained to function beneath his power for the benefit of a less powerful being. Women who are under the influence of small men are trained to submit like that.

Though the prophet Jeremiah was not a woman, he provides us with some insight about insecurity. Jeremiah started out as an inferior, scared little boy. God had to shake him out of his deception and awaken him to his true God-given power. As it says in Jeremiah 1:6-8,

Then said I, Ah, Lord God! behold, I cannot speak: for I am a child.

But the Lord said unto me, Say not, I am a child: for thou shalt go to all that I shall send thee, and whatsoever I command thee thou shalt speak.

Be not afraid of their faces: for I am with thee to deliver thee, saith the Lord.

Jeremiah was always a powerful prophet but he was conditioned to miniaturize himself compared to the world. He did not get this idea of inferiority from God. He didn't make it up. Where did it come from? He was told that he was a child. There was some human contamination. People told him he was a child and couldn't speak. What have people told you? Could it be possible that you are much greater on the inside than you are presently projecting? *Absolutely!*

THREE REASONS FOR INSECURITY

1. Self-Concocted Limitations Create Insecurity.
The first thing that Jeremiah said was, "I cannot speak." This was untrue because clearly he was speaking when he said he couldn't speak. Whenever life challenges us to actualize the power and potential within our minds, we create excuses for why we can't do it.

> *A queen finds solutions, while a*
> *weak woman finds excuses.*

Most of the things you are afraid of don't exist anywhere but in your mind. Every woman should take the time to think about her fears. They may be phantom phobias.

I remember when I was a child there was a popular pest control company named Miller the Killer. They had a black and white television commercial that ran frequently. In this commercial there was a big roach that would stand upright on its hind legs. In one of the commercials, the roach wore what looked like a long trench coat. One night, after a full evening of television and the lights were out, I was in bed and I just knew I saw a big Miller the Killer roach standing on the other side of the room. It was about seven feet tall and was about four feet wide. I screamed for my dad. When he turned on the light it was just his coat hanging on the closet door. I concocted a threat in my own mind based on what was deposited into my subconscious mind. I learned that night to verify before reacting. Every woman would do wonders for her personal advancement if she verified before she drew conclusions about life and her capacity. Don't be the victim of yourself.

> *"It is better to reach for the moon and come up short than to reach for the ground and hit it every time."* —Author Unknown

2. A Poor Self-View Ignites Insecurity.

Jeremiah defined himself as a child. The question is, how did Jeremiah know he was a child? The answer is, somebody told him. Therefore, Jeremiah's self-definition wasn't even his own perspective. His self-perspective amounted to what was spoken into him by others. Who has given you your self-perspective? Were they accurate?

> *Most women's self-definitions are not based on personal revelation; rather, they simply repeat the opinions of others.*

Jeremiah was telling himself what he heard others say about him. The beautiful thing about the Jeremiah story is that God eventually gave Jeremiah His definition of who He had made Jeremiah to be. God said to Jeremiah, "You are a prophet." God went so far as to tell Jeremiah to stop saying that he was a child. Every woman should pray to hear God's voice about His perspective. After all, according to the late Dr. Myles Monroe, *The only one that has the right to define anything is the creator of the thing.* The product itself doesn't have the right to define itself. A queen will never allow the world to label her. She is labeled and limited by God's view alone.

*Many women struggle in their identity
because of body shaming.*

The world will promote a certain body type as beauty, and every woman begins to attempt to modify her physical makeup to get as close to that shallow, external standard as possible. Black women for generations have tried to lighten their skin and thin their naturally-rounded hips because mainstream standards of beauty typically have only shown thin, white women as beautiful. In recent times, the hip-hop movement has used music videos to promote a more urban, ethnic brand of beauty. This message says: A woman must have wide hips, small waist, and a very large bottom. Consequently, white women are getting injections and implants to create an anatomy that the Creator never intended for them. Why don't women—black, white, and other—simply love the bodies God gave them? They are all being managed by a system that shames them into spending billions annually to achieve what is often ana-tomically unachievable.

A woman who lives with body shame is also more sexually compliant, just to have the affections of a man. It's a misogynistic game. A man will directly or indirectly degrade a woman's physical attributes to lure her into the trap of his approval, and then he will manipulate her into sexual situations she never saw coming. When a woman's queen-consciousness awakens, she is not moved by the pointless and useless opinions of any person or system.

*A queen looks in the mirror and falls in love
with exactly what God has given her.*

No matter what your body type is, there is a wise and loving king somewhere waiting for a queen that fits your exact profile. He will love every inch of you exactly as God has designed you. If he cannot love you as you presently are, his love will fail not too far into the future. What will happen when time changes your features? There are only so many plastic surgery procedures a woman may do. If a man cannot completely love you at your current weight and shape, he does not love you.

I was watching the popular talk show *The Real* and they were discussing body shaming. One of the hosts said that she has cellulite and she wasn't afraid to admit it. She then went on to say that she discovered men that actually loved her cellulite. The women found that hard to believe, but as a full-grown man I can testify that men are attracted to much of what women detest. You are beautiful beyond your imagination, my dear daughter.

3. Fear of Opinions Feeds Insecurity.
Another prominent cause of personal insecurity is the fear of people and what they might think. Jeremiah was also troubled by what other people might think of him. God said to him, "Don't be afraid of their faces." From this we may deduce that Jeremiah was overly concerned with the reactions of people. This translates into the insecurities of many women. There's an unreal anxiety that comes over many women when they feel as though the public may not approve.

Average women are too focused on how other people see them and find themselves intimidated by the possibility of disapproval.

The psalmist puts it best in Psalm 118:6, *The Lord is on my side; I will not fear: what can man do unto me?* Who do you really have to fear when you know that God is for you? The word of God declares, *If God be for us, who can be against us?* (Romans 8:31).

Why be insecure or intimidated about people when God is on your team?

> *One of the characteristics of a queen is that she manages her mind when it comes to obsessing over things that don't matter.*

Big women are not captured by small matters and don't entertain things that don't empower. A queen must take responsibility for her toxic thinking. You can give your power away if you don't think about what you're thinking about. Just one idea of insufficiency or an inkling of inferiority can rob a person of a very pivotal destiny moment. Many times, we are our own worst enemies. This was the case with the Children of Israel when they got to the Promised Land. They sent in spies, and the spies measured themselves by the inhabitants of the land, concluding that they were as grasshoppers in their own sight. So, they believed they were mere grasshoppers in the sight of the Canaanites as well (Numbers 13:33).

Quite often, it is our own personal insecurities that make us feel like other people are viewing us negatively. But, it is not them, we are the ones who really have the problem. A queen confronts all insecurity and negativity.

A queen realizes that personal insecurity is a liability to ruling and reigning. People may impose themselves into your life if you can't manage your own mind. Insecurity provides the world with the buttons to your soul. People

who do not mean you well may gain control of your life
when you tolerate insecurity.

> *There are some things that can only be
> eliminated by the woman herself. When
> her thinking is draining her power,
> she must eliminate that thinking.*

Insecurity is a product of poor thought patterns. There are
no external solutions to what is going on inside of your
head. There are but two individual's that can alter your
thinking and they are you and God. In fact, God cannot do
anything about your thinking until you take the initiative
to extract the root of the problem. The Bible calls these
negative and debilitating thought patterns "strongholds."
    The Bible states in 2 Corinthians 10:4-5,

> *For the weapons of our warfare are not carnal,
> but mighty through God to the pulling down of
> strong holds;*
>
> *Casting down imaginations, and every high thing
> that exalteth itself against the knowledge of God,
> and bringing into captivity every thought to the
> obedience of Christ.*

The text says that the stronghold should be pulled down.
This speaks of dismantling the thoughts that produce the
negative effects.

    The practical application, of this text, is that the woman
should scan every thought before reacting and cancel the
thoughts that bring her down. Those thoughts that lean
towards worry about people and their issues must be disposed of immediately.

HOW DOES A QUEEN ATTACK INSECURITY?

1. A Queen Must Force Her Life out of Every Comfort Zone.
You attack insecurity by living your life, day to day, outside of the comfortable range of what you're familiar with. A queen never allows herself to become stagnant. She is always pushing herself to be greater. This process can become very frightening, but it is mandatory for the woman intent on maximizing her life. *You can't go to where you're going by staying where you are.* Push through your insecurities and discover the next dimension.

*Insecurity will never leave quietly—
it must be cast out forcefully.*

You will discover that insecurity is extremely possessive and won't let go easily. The only way to extract insecurity is by force. It will require the forceful management of your personal standard and never settling for less.

*Insecurity likes to live under the
darkness of internalization.*

The insecure woman tends to cover it up. She may use things like designer clothing and flawless makeup to hide beneath. These are simply futile efforts to disguise her fright and timidity.

*I call this process "mascara therapy"—she's
attempting to paint away the painful truth.*

Insecurity must be exposed to the light of honesty before it can be disposed of.

2. A Queen Must Forgive.

One of the most deceptive forms of insecurity and negativity is the unwillingness to forgive. It is deceptive because we may genuinely feel entitled to maintaining this cancerous emotion within our souls. We may feel justified in holding on to bitterness toward a disloyal lover or an absent father. The thing that escapes us is that the impact of the bitterness is eroding the foundation of our core. You cannot be whole and complete with an unforgiving spirit dominating your soul.

> *Unforgiveness at its base is a form of insecurity. It is the fear of trusting again for fear of disappointment or injury.*

It takes a great deal of effort to hold on to bitterness and anger. Why do people maintain their positions of animosity? They are really afraid to release and move on for fear of being made a fool. While they are so concerned about their image, they fail to see that their core is being destroyed. It would be the equivalent of a woman who is more concerned about her hair than her lungs.

One need only turn on cable television to observe any of the plethora of female-based reality shows to see that too many women retain negativity in their souls, like a mother coddling her newborn. If reality shows are beneath you, just go to almost any church in America and observe some of the women in leadership. You will soon discover that many of them are petty and messy. They are often gossipers and the breeders of contention. They are jealous of each other and do not celebrate their individual or collective value. If you are not a church person, just think about how many times at work when women are at the center of major dissension. Most of the time these confrontations are a backlash from issues that have been unresolved for years. Things that should have been settled with a simple adult conversation creep way too far into the future and abort the woman's promotion moment. The time that she should be advancing in her career goals and her relationships, she is still floundering like a novice. This is all too often the consequence of toxic waste poisoning her system.

> *Unforgiveness keeps the woman*
> *functioning in pettiness.*

When a woman truly develops her queen cognizance, she becomes too big for petty tendencies. A queen realizes she has a kingdom to rule and does not lend herself to the exercises of a common woman. Her awareness of the weight of her identity and destiny puts a demand on her to keep her heart clean so that her head may be clear. She does not fabricate, nor does she retain negativity within her circle. She removes herself from everything negative.

> *A queen doesn't allow her ears, mind, or*
> *heart to become a trash can littered with past*
> *offenses and outdated bitterness. A queen*
> *disposes of the trash in pursuit of the treasure.*

The Bible admonishes us along these lines, *Ye therefore, beloved, seeing ye know these things before, beware lest ye also, being led away with the error of the wicked, fall from your own stedfastness* (2 Peter 3:17).

The world believes in holding grudges and bitterness

close to the heart; but, holding bitterness in your soul is like stashing a raw chicken breast out of sight behind the bookshelf. Though it is not seen, it will have a devastating impact on your life and environment. When you allow bitterness, unforgiveness, and anger to dwell in your heart, you are defiling your own life.

> *As a queen, you can't allow your*
> *future to be miniaturized by failing to*
> *process negativity expeditiously.*

When we look at Queen Esther, we clearly see that she had to detox in preparation for her royal ascension. This was a physical cleansing of the body in preparation for her encounter with the king.

Esther 2:12 records the encounter,

> *Now when the turn of each maiden came to*
> *go in to King Ahasuerus, after the regulations*
> *for the women had been carried out for twelve*
> *months—since this was the regular period for*
> *their beauty treatments, six months with oil of*
> *myrrh and six months with sweet spices and*
> *perfumes and the things for the purifying of the*
> *women . . . (AMPC).*

Though Esther's process was physical, it can symbolize a spiritual and emotional process that every modern queen must experience. To have your moment of royal elevation, you must purge from anything and everything that leaves the residue of past pain and previous toxicity.

> *You cannot bring garbage into the palace.*

To detox will require a specific approach to living that is designed to eliminate everything from the queen's soul that does not agree with her destiny, productivity, and ultimate happiness.

I was once attempting to engage a certain social media platform by way of a live video message. As I attempted to start the stream, my smart phone read, "Not enough space." It was indicating that I needed to delete some of the things that were previously installed in my memory before I could move forward with my present plans.

> *A queen must never allow her future to be kidnapped by the past. She must delete the things that incumber her vision.*

The first step towards the purging of the royal soul is forgiveness. Women are so severely and abundantly abused and wounded by life, men, and society that they struggle with moving on. They are not only insecure, they are broken. When she has been continually beaten down and abused by people who were supposed to protect and cultivate her, she becomes callused.

Most women are put off by the idea of forgiveness because there is a huge misunderstanding of what forgiveness really is. To gain some perspective of what forgiveness is, let's take a glimpse at what forgiveness is not. *Forgiveness is not the diminishing of the pain you've incurred. Forgiveness has nothing to do with justifying the wrong doer. Forgiveness does not demand that the forgiver opens her life and arms to the offender again.*

Forgiveness is choosing to leave every person that has wronged you in the hands of God and the past while you move on positively, confidently, peacefully, and successfully into your future.

Many women are literally so attached to painful events and hurtful people from their distant and recent past that they are emotionally and psychologically unavailable for present opportunities or any concept of destiny. She can't receive good people today because she is tied to the memories of the toxic people of yesterday. She is totally oblivious to the reality that her obsession with this person and event is putting her personal success and happiness on hold.

Forgiveness is the process whereby the soul eliminates emotional and spiritual free radicals, and it prevents the malignancy of bitterness from consuming the consciousness.

Ephesians 4:31 puts it this way:
> *Let all bitterness, and wrath, and anger, and clamour, and evil speaking, be put away from you, with all malice:*
>
> *And be ye kind one to another, tenderhearted, forgiving one another, even as God for Christ's sake hath forgiven you.*

Forgiveness is not a feeling—it is a personal decision and effort to eliminate any and everything that conflicts with your emotional and spiritual balance.

When you forgive, it is self-care. At the end of the day, people assume that forgiveness is a weak move made by women who are pushovers. The reality is this: the greatest gift a person may give herself is the forgiveness of her offenders.

The inability to forgive allows those who hurt you to travel into your future to exact even greater and perpetual pain.

The Apostle Paul reveals an interesting fact about the spiritual reality of not forgiving. He states in 2 Corinthians 2:10-11,

> *If you forgive anyone anything, I too forgive that one; and what I have forgiven, if I have forgiven anything, has been for your sakes in the presence [and with the approval] of Christ (the Messiah),*

> *To keep Satan from getting the advantage over us; for we are not ignorant of his wiles and intentions* (AMPC).

In common everyday terms, Paul is saying we must continue to make forgiveness our culture if we are to please Christ. He then states that forgiveness is necessary to prevent Satan from taking advantage of us.

When we don't forgive, we allow access to evil.

When a queen does not release the pain and anger about past events, she has to understand that she is not only battling the memories, she is also striving against demonic influence. *Satan uses the moment to create a psychological monument.* A queen's life must never be relegated to a monument of painful history; her life is always a movement to destiny.

3. A Queen Washes Her Brain.

The next step the conscious queen makes to eliminate the negativity is to wash her brain. The idea of brain-washing is generally frowned upon because it carries the connotation of being psychologically manipulated into becoming a robot of some kind at the behest of another. One person indoctrinates another for the purposes of control.

I'd like us to look at the idea of brain-washing from a different angle. Rather than the usual definition of one party manipulating the mind of another, let's see it as a person who has been indoctrinated with lies and deceit washing her brain of all of the propaganda.

A queen has to unlearn the lies.

The harsh reality for the women of the world is this: You have been conditioned to think beneath your royal status. It is through the intentional inferiority conditioning that the world makes slaves of monarchs. The queen has to wash her consciousness of all traces of slave-conditioning.

Every queen must recognize that it is vital to renew her thinking. There are ideas and thoughts she has about herself that must be eliminated from the soundtrack of her conscious and subconscious mind.

Every woman has a song that is on repeat in her soul. That song was either produced by the bad experiences of a cruel world, or it is the song of self-confidence and intentional empowerment that come of a positive outlook.

A queen must maintain a high level of thought about herself, others, and the world she lives in. A queen possesses an infectious positivity.

CHAPTER 6

QUEENS POSSESS PRESENCE

QUEEN-CONSCIOUSNESS
(A Queen Owns the Space She Is In)

*As King Paternam proceeded to go deeper into the ways of a queen with his young daughters, he shifted his instruction from the things that queens do to the way queens are. He talked to his daughters about one word: **presence**. The king said, "When a queen enters a room, her regal presence demands respect. When a queen appears, all eyes follow her; her presence commands and fills the space." He explained to the young royals that presence is the identification mark of true queens. Queens never need to fight for attention because they possess the gift of presence.*

The king lamented the fact that their mother, the late queen, was no longer alive to model what he was trying to teach, so he summoned the best illustration he could find. He brought the young girls to the palace zoo. When they got there, he walked them over to the lion's cage. As they looked at the lion and the lion looked back, the king asked, "Would anyone like to go in with the lion?"

Each girl emphatically cried, "No way!"

"Why?"

"The lion is not to be played with."

"How do you know? Has he ever done anything to you?"

"No, he hasn't, but we can look in his eyes and tell that we should stay here."

*"**Bingo!**" the king exclaimed. "The lion doesn't have to do anything but just be and everyone in his vicinity knows what he is and what are his capabilities. This is because the lion has a certain presence. Everything about the lion speaks of his being king of the jungle. When the lion is on the prowl, everything else gets out of the way. Likewise, a queen speaks before she opens her mouth. Like the lion, **a queen has presence**."*

For many women, the concept of *presence* is foreign, or at least ill-defined. Most will conclude that presence is simply being in a space; but, to be in a space is simply to be "in a space." Light fixtures are in spaces, but few are ever consciously noticed. It is important to understand the concept of presence.

To have presence is to own the space you're in.

A queen owns her space. She has a unique ability to circumvent drama and overshadow petty mediocrity in order to politely reign over any environment with grace and class.

She is never loud or brash, yet she drowns out every voice in a room. Her silence is more penetrating than a fool's rant. A queen's walk is poetic and mesmerizing. It is not sexual or enticing—it is captivating and regal. A queen's disposition says that she is in another league, and yet her humility and ability to assimilate makes all feel as equals. Her manners and smile make all feel better about themselves. Her presence makes the environment brighter.

As I write this, I have just left London, England. While there, the locals enjoyed telling stories of a beautiful princess who died too young. Her name was Diana. I remember the young, beautiful, and compassionate Diana, Princess of Wales. She was the first wife of Charles, Prince of Wales. She died tragically in 1997 at the hands of over-aggressive photographers seeking photos to sell. As they were in pursuit of her car, she suffered a fatal car crash.

I can remember how this young royal possessed something that captured the attention of the entire world. Some say that it was her exquisite beauty. And though she was beautiful, it had to be more; there had been beautiful royals who had pre-dated her, and yet they did not garner

the magnetism she possessed. This lady was revered and adored worldwide. There was something about her presence that overshadowed even her royal in-laws. Diana could take a still photograph and there would be something unexplainable reaching from the image into the heart of the viewer. Diana had presence.

> **When women understand the power and value of presence, they will begin to attract everything to themselves that they desire and deserve.**

A queen's presence is her internal energy. Presence is the overflow of essence—it fills a room before she ever says a word. Her presence is the silent voice of royalty. Her presence is like the look in the lion's eye before she roars. This is very important—*you will never manifest presence while living in a superficial state of mind.* Presence emanates from the spirit of the queen.

There's a record of a man who possessed presence which opened doors of favor for him. This is the biblical character named Daniel. Daniel was a foreigner in a volatile country, and yet there was something about him that captured the attention of the king.

> **When you have presence, you never need to fight for recognition.**

In Daniel 6:3 it states, *Then this Daniel was preferred above the presidents and princes, because an excellent spirit was in him; and the king thought to set him over the whole realm.*

It was not Daniel's performance that afforded him advancement, it was his presence. The king noticed his "excellent spirit." What was in him was drawing the right people to him. *Common women consistently use their most shallow attributes and attract the wrong people and circumstances.* A queen never attempts to draw attention. She just *is* and she attracts what she is.

A queen is more concerned about her core than she is her color or cut.

Presence starts with what is on the inside and then it progresses to an external reflection. A million-dollar look with a two-cent spirit will never produce the energy of presence. This is how a woman may be the most physically beautiful woman in the room and yet the most unattractive. There's no harmony between her core and her surface. She has no presence.

Presence is the connection between who you are, what the world sees of you, and what you consistently deliver.

When there's a breakdown in either of the three components just mentioned—who a woman is internally, what she projects to the world, and what she consistently delivers—her presence is compromised. There is nothing more commanding than a woman who walks into a room and knows who she is, projects her authentic self, and does it consistently under all conditions.

One of the things I so appreciated about the Obama presidency was the First Lady. Michelle Obama had presence. You could tell it was not an act and that she was perfectly comfortable in her own skin. She consistently maintained her presence for eight years. It didn't matter if she was being disrespected in the media or embracing world leaders, she always stood out in a room. Anyone watching would testify that it was impossible to not be drawn to her class, beauty, kindness, and dignity. She didn't just bring the physical beauty of a black queen to the scene, she brought intellect, wisdom, discretion, passion, and kindness to people who sometimes were not deserving of such virtues. I think one of the sayings she may be most remembered for is something she said during the 2016 presidential campaign: "When they go low, we always go high." Those words encapsulate the philosophical perspective of a queen—always raise the bar.

> *A queen always rises above the standard and resets the bar. A queen has presence. Your presence is how you're perceived without saying a word.*

Every generation of women seems to move further and further away from the concept of feminine grace. There was a time when etiquette classes were offered in schools, at church, local recreational centers, and even taught by mothers at home. Today, one has to be careful about suggesting to a woman the benefits of an etiquette class. A man, such as myself, might be accused of misogynistic intentions. The reality is this: a queen must be trained in the ways of queens. Even a queen by birth requires someone to tell her that she is a queen and to teach her how to walk as such.

The political climate today is so charged with disdain for the concept of femininity and the idea that a woman should possess a distinct presence from a man. Many get offended at the idea of a woman having a presence. I'm certain that there will be some who will lift this brief passage from this book and take issue with my suggestion. I will probably be accused of misogyny and being another middle-aged guy attempting to shackle new generations of women to antiquated values—in other words, an old man trying to imprison women to outdated concepts of femininity. I digress. Nevertheless, the truth remains, a queen should have an equal but distinct presence from a king.

A woman should have the right to do whatever she desires and is capable of doing well, but she should clearly be a woman.

I believe that a woman should be paid equally for equal work; however, I don't believe that she has to lose every semblance of her feminine presence to do so. Enough of my rant.

The start of greatness is in presence. The energy a person exudes establishes a corresponding atmosphere and attracts an equivalent return. When an entertainer has a confident presence, it attracts a receptive reaction from her audience. When a preacher has a powerful presence, it moves an entire congregation. When a queen has a feminine, strong, and regal presence, it moves kingdoms and makes kings' heads swivel. Much success may be traced back to presence.

THE POWER OF PRESENCE

There's a biblical example of the very real power of presence found in the life of King Solomon. The queen of Sheba visited his kingdom to hear his wisdom and to prove his reputation of being the greatest of all kings. When she arrived, she discovered that Solomon's kingdom and prominence was actually greater than what had been reported.

1 Kings 10:4-5 records the encounter of Sheba and Solomon:

> *And when the Queen of Sheba had seen all of Solomon's wisdom, and the house that he had built,*
>
> *And the meat of his table and the sitting of his servants, and the attendance of his ministers, and his apparel, and his cupbearers, and his ascent by which he went up into the house of the Lord; there was no more spirit in her.*

When the Queen of Sheba arrived at Solomon's palace, it was breathtaking. His presence was demonstrated in the dress of his servants and the order of his court. She saw his presence in his excellent manner of doing things.

Here's the beauty: She was blown away by his presence before he physically appeared. She was knocked off her feet before she actually met Solomon. His presence was in everything pertaining to him.

A queen's presence makes its arrival before she appears and remains after she exits.

Queen Sheba was so overwhelmed with awe that she fainted. The Bible says, *There was no more spirit in her.* Presence is not about making a scene. Presence is about authentic excellence and class. It is raising the standard in a room that most can only aspire to.

THE COMPONENTS OF A QUEEN'S PRESENCE

1. A Queen's Presence Starts with Her Self-Assurance.
Assurance is a certainty of one's own abilities or chances for success. The starting block of the queen's track to presence is assurance. The queen, who is in control of her power, is always self-assured. To be assured simply means that the queen is confident of who she is and what she possesses. A queen does not tolerate insecurity of any kind within herself. A queen possesses disdain for any inkling of a weak constitution. She attacks her insecurities with a vengeance until she has rid herself of all internal doubts and fears. The queen is so fortified within herself that the world may come against her with all that it possesses, and yet she will remain self-assured. The queen's mind does not process timidity or dejection. She will always rise above the turbulence of any moment because she always believes she can. *A queen is like a golfer—she doesn't need cheerleaders because their inner self-estimation is always sufficient to elevate their game.*

> **Insecurity is a beast that eats away
> at the core of greatness. It erodes the
> confidence necessary to rule.**

A queen ushers into any atmosphere an uncommon confidence. She makes women notice, and men are often intimidated by her unshakable self-assurance. Her presence says, "*I can't lose!*"

A queen is always self-assured because she understands she has the power of the entire kingdom at her disposal. Her assurance is not an exercise in vain girl-power—her confidence is rooted in who she knows she is, what she has, and who she knows is backing her up.

As a queen of the twenty-first century and beyond, you must find your assurance, not only in your personal power, but in the power of God that backs you up. As a queen, you will face a myriad of challenges and emotional foes that come to kill your self-esteem. Always remember what the scripture says about you.

One such text is Philippians 4:13 which declares: *I can do all things through Christ which strengtheneth me.* Another passage to hold close to your heart is found in 2 Timothy 1:7, which says, *For God hath not given us a spirit of fear; but of power, and of love, and of a sound mind.*

> *A queen always controls her thoughts and meditations to maintain her confidence. She must be assured of who she is.*

It is imperative that every woman answer the "Who am I?" question within her own heart according to her Creator's definition. If you do not find the answer to this vital question from within, an unfriendly world will redefine you and limit your true power to see yourself properly. *If you cannot see yourself, you will never produce presence. Presence always follows awareness.* The lion has such presence because she knows and believes in who she is. A queen has to know who she is and understand her worth. When she knows her true worth and value, she will generate a silent demand for that worth. A queen's awareness of her true value and identity is like a Rolls Royce sitting on a showroom floor. You can look through the window and know that this vehicle is extremely costly. When you know who you are, the world will discern your value and feel your presence.

A queen is a God original.

God did not make a pair of you. You are the Creator's original. When a queen understands this, she begins to exude a silent and humble confidence that will permeate every atmosphere. In a society filled with small and insecure women, a queen will walk into any room and own it with her quiet and unassuming boldness. Her presence is based in her assurance, and her assurance is steeped in the constant awareness of who she is in the Creator.

The psalmist puts this in very practical and yet poetic terms in Psalm 139:14, *I am fearfully and wonderfully made: marvelous are thy works; and that my soul knoweth right well.*

The writer describes himself as the creation of God. He says that he is fearfully and wonderfully made. Wow! The most significant part of the verse is not his description of the Creator's investment in him. The greatest and most significant part of the verse is where he testifies that his soul knows it. In other words, the psalmist is saying, *I am not just a walking treasure from Heaven, I am aware of who I am! I am not oblivious to my worth.* A queen is always keenly aware of who she is and the value she carries.

A queen must be assured of her territory.

A queen carries a certain assurance about the command of her space. A woman who possesses confidence is never intimidated by other strong women. Real queens welcome other queens into their palace. Why? Because at the end of the visit, it is her palace and her kingdom; all others are just visitors.

A queen is never intimidated by others who do well.

Queens don't fall victim to jealousies and paranoia. *A queen knows that her realm is on lock!* She is certain about her realm because she takes care of it. Her man, her children, her business, and all other matters are securely provided for by her regal wisdom and balance. At the end of each day, her business is all good because she has nurtured it.

> *A true queen understands that her crown
> and throne are tailor-made and engraved—
> nobody else can occupy her territory.*

When a woman walks into a space and knows that she owns it, the entire world takes notice. For instance, Oprah Winfrey has *owned television*, pun intended, for decades. Oprah has made mega-stars from her platform with no hesitation. If she were not a self-assured queen who knew her gifting and understood her realm, she might have been a typical jealous, little woman who fought to hold on to something that was completely hers. But because she knows her realm, she has been able to share it. A queen is never a petty and jealous little girl fighting over a doll. She is a full-grown woman who knows her power, understands her territory, and is never in doubt about the security of her empires.

For example, a queen is not running behind her man because she's afraid another woman is going to take him. A queen will take such good care of her man that she will have no fear of him leaving for another.

Proverbs 31:11 says of the virtuous woman, *The heart of her husband doth safely trust in her, so that he will have no need of spoil.* This woman took care of her wifely responsibilities so well that her husband had no excuse. When a queen has done her job, she can relax her mind. If things don't work out, it won't be because the queen failed to cover her territory. Furthermore, because the queen does such a great job of caring for her king, she won't struggle to relieve him of his duties if he proves to be less than a man of honor. A queen does not beg a man to be loyal; she will instead move on rather quickly. A queen will banish a man from the royal palace swiftly.

She must be assured of her competence.

A queen knows that she can perform competently when necessary. She does not carry a spirit of self-doubt, but she believes in her ability to do the job. If she does not understand all of the particulars, she knows that she can learn how to do it and will not relent until she has mastered it.

When a woman walks into any setting with a mind that she can do the job, she shifts the atmosphere. The world is so accustomed to intimidating women by using the threat of tasks that it views as beyond or above her. *But when the woman displays a personal confidence in her own competence, she disrupts the ecosystem of misogyny and male chauvinism.* In other words, she creates a problem for the male-dominated society that might seek to miniaturize her true greatness because only a *true king* can appreciate a queen who can do the job, believe she can do the job, and actually get it done. Kings will stand and applaud. Every king realizes he needs a queen like this.

Competence carries a distinct presence.

In many instances, single sisters are troubled about the lack of attention coming from average men. If the sister will observe the profiles of the majority of these men, she would discover that they are average or below in terms of vision, ambition, work ethic, spiritual maturity, and-leadership skills.

> *Average men are always intimidated*
> *by the mere presence of a queen.*

Average men are not deep enough to settle on a woman who is assured of her own competence. A woman of lesser self-esteem might suit the shallow purposes of most men better. *A queen should take it as a compliment that average men won't approach.* Her presence is too much. The queen is like the sun—there's a desire to embrace her but her brilliance is too much to bear.

2. A Queen's Presence Is Married to Her Attitude.
A queen's presence is also hinged on a distinct attitude. The unique thing about a true queen is that she can dine with royals one evening and walk with common everyday people in the marketplace the next morning. The woman of Proverbs 31 was wealthy and humble all at the same time. She had an attitude that ingratiated her to people from all walks of life.

Let's pause for Q & A—What is your attitude like on a daily basis? What do the people closest to you say about your attitude? Have you recently drawn positive people to you because of your intentional attitude?

> *Nothing makes a more brilliant impression*
> *than a powerful woman walking into a*
> *room without pretension or insecurity,*
> *but with a balanced and warm spirit.*

A queen is not arrogant or insecure, she's just authentic. She's not excited by the things she has, nor is she envious of the things others have. She's just her authentic self at all times. She doesn't think herself better than anyone else, and certainly does not perceive that she is less than anyone, either. A queen's attitude is pleasant and balanced.

A queen knows how to be polite
and yet establish boundaries.

A queen projects her attitude through her speech. She uses the appropriate words to create a climate of respect for others and herself. She makes everybody feel bigger and better by her words and simultaneously she extinguishes any foolery that might be directed at her.

The Bible says in Proverbs 31:26, *She openeth her mouth with wisdom; and in her tongue is the law of kindness.*

A woman who knows what to say,
when to say it, and how to say it will be
unforgettable and indispensable.

The Bible states in Proverbs 15:1, *A soft answer turneth away wrath: but grievous words stir up anger.* A queen can turn a volatile climate into a cordial encounter through her intentional words.

The most radiant aspect of a
woman is her attitude.

It is quite amazing how quickly a physically attractive woman may become unattractive when her attitude is poor. On the flip side, a woman who may possess average features but has an extraordinary attitude, becomes a superstar. The world will bow and make available all of its resources for the queen who has a pleasant and loving attitude. A woman's attitude paints every environment with her essence. A wise woman uses her attitude to shift the world around her.

A queen has power, but she walks in humility. She wears power well. She's never excited about success or promotion. She always keeps her attitude steady and balanced. Proverbs 22:4 says, *By humility and the fear of the Lord are riches, and honour, and life.*

> *A queen succeeds in life and business*
> *because she maintains humility,*
> *which is the posture of honor.*

The place of honor is the position of special favor and commendation. A queen, because of her humble and genuine nature, always reserves the top spot in the eyes of power brokers as well as everyday people. Her rise is due to her willingness to stay low.

3. A Queen Uses Her Attire to Project Her Presence.

A queen always observes a particular dress code. You'll notice, if you pay attention, that queens, and royals in general, are rarely dressed in a trendy sense. A queen especially has a dress code that sets standards. She does not take her cue from Hollywood or mainstream society. A queen dresses to start trends, never to follow them.

> *A queen's dress code is the*
> *preview of her presence.*

She uses her attire to forecast her essence. A queen's dress code speaks to her character, her objectives, her power, and her state of mind.

A queen dresses with the intention of making a statement. She never dresses to garner random attention, but to project power.

For instance, a "conscious queen" *(a woman who knows her worth)* would never be found wearing a dress that's fighting to expose her most private parts. A queen does not go naked in public. She is never mistaken as a woman so out of touch with her value that she uses her sexuality as a calling card. *A queen dresses on purpose, for a purpose.*

I remember when Michelle Obama appeared on a particular late-night show. The host asked her if her ensemble was a very expensive designer's original. She politely corrected him and said that her outfit was from a popular moderately-priced store. Because she is a five-star woman, she added value to the garment. It was a modestly-priced ensemble, but it represented who she was at her core. She dressed like a proud black woman who had earned degrees from some of the most prestigious institutions in the world. She was dressed like the wife of the POTUS (President of The United States). What would have happened if she had walked onto that stage with some of the stuff we all too often see women wearing today? I don't need to get specific; we all have the visual.

A queen uses her attire to announce her presence visually.

When you think of the ultimate version of yourself as a woman, does your wardrobe point to the ultimate version of you? Who are you dressing for? What are you attempting to accomplish by the way you dress? If you answer these questions honestly, you may have a major key to accelerating your power as a woman. Your choice of clothing is either enlarging or miniaturizing your public persona.

A queen dresses like she belongs to a king.

The Bible says in Proverbs 31:22-23, *She maketh herself coverings of tapestry; her clothing is silk and purple. Her husband is known in the gates . . .*

This woman covered herself intentionally. Her husband was a prominent man in society and his wife dressed like she belonged to him. A queen always dresses like she has a king somewhere. Many women seeking eligible men miss the boat because they are not dressing to project their presence. A queen does not wait to have a king in hand to dress like a wife. The wise queen understands that she must dress like a wife to be discovered as a wife.

4. A Queen Has the Audacity to Take Ownership of Any Environment.

Another aspect of the queen's presence is her audacity (or *fearlessness, boldness,* and *bravery*). A queen has the nerve to actually be queen under all conditions. Don't misunderstand—she's not brash and overbearing; rather, she is definitely going to enforce her rights and exercise her powers. She's not necessarily aggressive, but she is always assertive. A queen is not a coward or a pushover. She knows who she is and will make certain that you too recognize it and know what she deserves.

A queen has an uncommon boldness
laced with grace and femininity.

When a queen has a worthy agenda and clear vision, she lets nothing prevent the execution of it. She has the audacity to even offend certain people or establishments to accomplish her mission.

There's a biblical record of a woman who had the audacity to break rules to manifest her purpose. It is found in Luke 7:37-38:

> *And, behold, a woman in the city, which was a sinner, when she knew that Jesus sat at meat in the Pharisee's house, brought an alabaster box of ointment,*

> *And stood at his feet behind him weeping, and began to wash his feet with tears, and did wipe them with the hairs of her head, and kissed his feet, and anointed them with the ointment.*

There are a few things we must lift from this woman's experience. I already know that certain people might ask, "How does this woman relate, in any way, to a queen? She was a sinner." It's true that she had a soiled reputation and a less than stellar history. Nevertheless, she was a queen in the estimation of her Creator. A queen is never at the mercy of society to give her a sense of identity. To the world, she may look to be only a bruised and battered woman, but in the mind of God she is a brilliant ruler in complete dominion of the territories He has assigned to her hand.

A queen is a queen, even if she's broken.

Furthermore, the woman of the text demonstrated the

kind of tenacity and audacity that becomes a queen. This woman did not allow restrictive, chauvinistic rules to deter her from her mission. She was not supposed to break into a private meeting with men as she did, but she did it anyway. She did not allow the opinions of society to constrict her determination. While they saw her as nothing more than a sinner, this lady did not consider their opinions as important when it came to her objectives. She was so focused, she had no shame. Finally, she had the audacity to be her authentic self before a critical crowd. They slandered her for her past mistakes and even scolded her for offering such expensive oil. None of this prevented her from being her authentic self. She poured the oil, cried tears onto Jesus' feet, and dried them with her hair. This woman had the audacity to be herself in a situation that might have forced a woman of a weaker constitution to alter her behavior to appease an angry society. This woman possessed the audacity that created presence. She commanded the moment, and the reward was that she attracted Jesus' attention.

When a queen enters the room, everyone can feel her sense of purpose. Her focus becomes magnetic in that it attracts certain people to her, and repels certain others.

> *The world is not always ready for a queen who has the audacity to rule. Don't be alarmed.*

One of the consequences of presence is that it generates a sense of intimidation in those who encounter the power of the queen. Quite often, a queen is under the impression that people do not like her or view her unfavorably. The reality is that many times a queen is feared because her presence raises the bar to a place that many do not believe they can reach. She is a misfit because she is a standout.

One of my spiritual daughters is Dr. Sonja Stribling of Atlanta, Georgia. Sonja is known as a "builder of women." Sonja is one of the premier life coaches in America.

One day, she asked me how could she tone her strong personality down. I told her that it would be impossible for her to tone it down because it is impossible for an eagle not to intimidate anything other than an eagle. There's nothing an eagle can do to not intimidate others. When a woman has the strong presence of a queen, people will often become uneasy.

A queen will even find it a challenge to make and maintain friendly relationships with most women because they will become so captivated by her fierceness that they won't connect with her humility and sincerity. People shy away from a queen out of respect and not necessarily reproach. Therefore, a queen's walk can be lonely and difficult.

This sense of intimidation also presents itself in the area of a queen's romantic relationships. There are not a lot of men who are totally comfortable with a queen. Average men are shaken by her drive and focus and view her standard as a personal reflection on his manhood. He is not big enough to accommodate her and he knows it. Her greatness will always eclipse his lack of self-confidence.

*Queens do not have a multitude of men
calling on them because most men
do not view themselves as measuring
up. Her presence silences men. It takes
a true king to call on a queen.*

CHAPTER 7

QUEENS ONLY HEAR KINGS

QUEEN-CONSCIOUSNESS
(Walk Like a Queen and Kings Will Follow)

*As King Paternam moved into teaching the young princesses about romance, he made one thing very clear—**queens never chase kings**, and they certainly do not entertain peasants! The king said to his young daughters, "When a queen walks like a queen, kings always follow. Common women seek the attention of kings, but kings are drawn to the presence of queens. Kings will only notice queens, and queens can only hear the call of kings. Just walk like a queen, and a king will find you."*

The king proceeded to teach the girls what kings were made of and how a true queen could only follow a king. Anything less would be unacceptable.

Their father described some of the attributes of true kings: "Kings are well-disciplined in the manner of honoring queens. Kings are responsible and decisive men who have answers for problems, and they are strong under pressure."

When the king was finished having this father-to-daughter talk, his girls' eyes gleamed with the excitement of enlightenment.

The greatest detriment to women today is a total lack of self-awareness. When you don't know who you are, you allow people into your space who shouldn't even be in your world. How many women are there whose lives have been ruined by illicit and unequal relationships with the opposite sex? As a spiritual father to women around the world, I can tell you that poor relationship choices is one of the leading reasons a queen forfeits her throne and loses her crown.

A conscious queen is programmed to respond to the voice of a king only.

When a woman hears, or even desires to hear, the voices of random men who may be lacking in character, vision, and ambition, she has to understand that she is deficient in her soul. When a woman is sufficiently cognizant of her own power and station, her frequency is elevated to a royal standard. She can't connect to any man less than a king. They may call, but she can't hear them.

A queen is sometimes viewed as socially difficult or anti-social. She is really not that complicated—she will not waste time, and she already knows that nothing less than a king will do.

A queen wants a king! If you're not a king, you need not apply for the job.

The beauty about a queen is that she may be perfectly content with ruling the kingdom until a proper king arrives. No queen falls into the relationship abyss because she is simply desperate for a man. Instead, she is so engaged in her own life, invested in her clear future, and enjoying her present accomplishments that if a king never arrives she knows her life will have been lived to the fullest. A king is simply a compliment to a life already well-lived.

A queen is not desperate, she is self-sufficient.

A queen appreciates the value of a collaboration and the power that could come from connecting with a worthy man, but she will never settle for a man who is not equivalent to her. Average women are plagued with a cultural conditioning that they are only worth something when a man is present. He may or may not be worthy, she just wants the image of a man. This is a self-destructive, anti-queen mindset. For a woman to accept a man who is insufficient would be like buying a car without an engine and parking it in the driveway. You may wash and wax it, but the reality is that it's there only to impress your neighbors.

A queen could never follow anyone less than a king. A lesser man could not command her respect.

The virtuous woman of Proverbs 31 had businesses, staff, charity outreaches, and she dressed like a queen. Another lesson for modern queens is that she had a husband she could relate to and respect. She was not married to a man of lesser station or philosophy. She didn't have a man who lacked equivalent motivation.

A woman of strength and drive cannot be saddled with an inferior.

The text says in Proverbs 31:23, *Her husband is known in the [city's] gates, when he sits among the elders of the land* (AMPC). She had a comparable husband. This, in part, is why the Apostle Paul encouraged people to be equally yoked. This is no reference to race; rather, an equal yoke is a relationship that is balanced spiritually, intellectually, emotionally, financially, and in temperament. The Bible states in Deuteronomy 22:10, *Thou shalt not plow with an ox and an ass together.*

One cannot expect to accomplish anything with a union between two species that are fundamentally opposite.

*A queen would fool herself to think
that she may leave the palace and
find a husband in the junkyard.*

The reality is this: you may be attracted to a person on a certain level, but a royal marriage requires equality. Too many women attempt to create kings from clowns. I've heard it said, "A crown on a clown does not make a king." When a woman is self-deficient, she reaches for men who are beneath her and makes pet projects of them. This is unfair to the men and a massive waste of time for her. If there is no basic compatibility in the subsurface levels of the two persons, it is futile.

The word of God says in Amos 3:3, *Can two walk together, except they be agreed?* When a queen's intelligence says, "This is not working," and her spirit says, "God has more for you," the queen shuts the relationship down. A queen will never sit a bum on a throne.

Who's sitting on your throne? A true king will come with his own throne and kingdom to match. A true king's proposition to the queen is the formation of a power couple.

A QUEEN ONLY HEARS A KING

1. There Are Certain Men That a Queen Never Considers.

A true queen is insulated from the riff-raff. She does not make apologies for constructing her life in a way that avoids the kind of man who does not measure up. A queen is not going to subject herself and her kingdom to the oversight of an inferior. How can a queen put a billion dollar economy into the hands of a man who doesn't even have a job, and doesn't want one?

2. A Queen will Never Claim a Weak Man.

The very basic aspects of female-to-male attraction are based in a man possessing a sense of strength and stability. A queen never looks for a man she has to emotionally and physically support every day. Of course, with the ebbs and flows of relationships, it is understandable that there will be times when he will lean on her; however, this is not to be the ongoing norm. The man is going to need to exude a strength that a strong woman can admire.

As the Bible puts it in 1 Peter 3:7, *Likewise, ye husbands, dwell with them according to knowledge, giving honour unto the wife, as unto the weaker vessel.* What's the message here? Is it that the woman is a helpless inferior? Not at all. The principle that is being conveyed in this most wise text is that the wife shouldn't be stronger than the husband. A wise woman looks for a man who is at least comparable in strength, emotionally, intellectually, and spiritually. The strength of the man is significant for the ongoing chemistry of the relationship.

*When a woman is stronger than her man
in certain areas, the chemistry of the
relationship eventually spins out of balance.*

A queen's assertive temperament dictates that she must have a man of considerable resolve, wisdom, and decisiveness. She would soon become emotionally disconnected from anything less.

3. A Queen Never Submits to a Controlling Man.

One thing that is very important to mention as we continue to look at a queen's choices regarding the selection of a king is that a strong man does not feel the need to control his woman. A truly strong man is secure enough to allow his woman to expand without fear or intimidation.

*A weak man attempts to exert control
over a woman's entire life.*

A real queen will never tolerate a controlling man! Too many women settle for men who feel the necessity to dictate their friendships, dress code, phone calls, and even their interaction with family and friends. This man is not a king, but a controller. A king doesn't control his queen, because a true king is quite content in his position and he respects his queen as his equal. The main reason he made her his queen is because he trusts her judgement. He has no desire or need to control her. They are equal partners in dominion.

The Bible shares a vital piece of wisdom for men in the rest of 1 Peter 3:7:

> *Likewise, ye husbands, dwell with them
> according to knowledge, giving honour unto the*

> *wife as unto the weaker vessel, and as being heirs*
> *together of the grace of life; that your prayers be*
> *not hindered.*

The text says that the man and the woman are "heirs together of grace." This is God's revelation of the power couple. A true king understands that the queen is a gift, not a servant or possession. No queen will ever submit to control, because control is abuse and disrespect.

> ### *A queen can submit to a true king, but will*
> ### *never be subjugated by a little tyrant.*

When the Bible admonishes the wife to submit to her husband, there is more being communicated than meets the eye. Before submission comes, the man must first demonstrate the qualities of a husband. He has to honor, protect, provide, and respect. Until these demands are met, he is not worthy of submission; therefore, submission is the natural response of the queen to the love and respect of the king. Kings do not have to control. A king's honor of the queen extracts respect from her. Respect is the seed that must be sown to reap the fruit of submission.

4. A Queen Never Accepts a Lazy Man.

In today's culture, it is not uncommon to see women providing for physically grown men as if they were children. What's worse is that we have such a pitiful segment of men in our culture that they are comfortable sitting and watching the woman do all of the earning and fighting for a future. She goes to school. She gets the job. She has the plans and works the plans while he sits and is kept.

> ### *A queen never supports grown, able men!*

If you are a woman and are considering financing a lazy man, you should use those resources to have your head examined! No woman in her right mind will allow a man to use her while he sits uselessly by. It is a reflection on a woman to allow a man to manipulate her financially. A queen has financial expectations of her king.

The Bible is direct about the issue of men who can work and won't. It states in 2 Thessalonians 3:10, *if any would not work, neither should he eat.*

Queens do not enable the arrested development of lazy non-working men. Of course, a queen will hold a real man down during hard times until he gets back on his feet, but a true queen would never lie next to a grown man who does not love her and her children enough to exert some energy to provide for them.

A queen has nothing in common with a slothful man. A sloth is an animal that is so lazy it sleeps most of its life away. A man does not have to make as much money as a queen, but he must bring a superior effort to the table. No woman can respect a man who can provide and chooses not to. At some point, this breakdown of basic relational roles will deteriorate the woman's chemistry with the man.

A queen does not mind ruling when she wants to, but when she does not feel up to it, she has to know her king is ready, willing, and able.

5. A Queen Does Not Tolerate an Unfaithful Man.

So many women are stuck in cycles of infidelity and don't understand why they continue to settle for it. I believe, as a pastor and father, that it stems from the lack of paternal impartation. In other words, the fathers have often been absent physically and/or emotionally. This has robbed the woman of a developed self-esteem. Father's establish the self-esteem of their daughters. When a woman has not had this paternal deposit, she searches for the approval of any male figure. Too often she finds a pseudo (fake) affirmation from a man who is simply playing games. This leads to her getting trapped in cycles of cheating and webs of lies. If she is not rescued, this may go on for a lifetime.

When the queen in the woman is awakened, she will no longer tolerate any man who does not make her first without a second in reserve.

Queens do not settle for anything less than fidelity. If a man cannot or chooses not to be faithful, she will banish him from the kingdom. A lesser, weaker woman would tolerate embarrassment and even jeopardize her health and life for a man who makes promises but no changes. But a queen does not share—everything is exclusive. 1 Corinthians 7:4 puts it this way: *The wife hath not power of her body, but the husband: and likewise also the husband hath not power of his own body, but the wife.*

Queens have their own man without sharing.

6. A Queen Vets Potential Kings through Intentional Questioning.

A major shift in the mindset of a woman who has developed her queen-consciousness is revealed in her approach to engaging men. The average woman usually floats along and believes everything a man says, most of which is a gross misrepresentation of the actual truth. Men have an uncanny propensity to present alternative facts. Alternative facts are the ideas that he wants the woman to believe, even though these facts are really fabrications or prevarications. In other words, the brother is lying.

If the woman does not have a relentless
system to prove a man, she will find herself
entertaining multiple failed relationships.

A queen has too much to lose to create intimate relationships based on anything but solid information. She
slows her heart down when it is attempting to fall for an
unproven man. Her head intervenes and says, "Let's think
this through." As a consequence, the queen is filled with
questions for any potential suitor.

A queen is wise enough to interrogate any so-called
king. She does not take anybody at their word. President
Ronald Reagan famously said of the Russians, "Trust, but
verify *(Doveryai, no poveryai)."* So a queen will ask questions to give the man a chance to prove his worthiness. An
average woman might be more likely to believe anything
without a cross-examination, but not a queen.

This point is demonstrated by the queen of Sheba
when she went to meet King Solomon. The queen had
heard many great things about Solomon, but she was too
wise to believe the hype without proving it to herself. Her
approach to testing the king was to ask questions. In fact,
she asked tough questions to prove him. The Bible records
it in 1 Kings 10:1, *And when the queen of Sheba heard of*
the fame of Solomon concerning the name of the Lord, she
came to prove him with hard questions.

A queen tests kings through questioning
because a queen can ask questions
that only kings can answer.

A queen's questions will reveal the motives, agendas, and
character of the man. Just like Solomon, only a king has

answers to hard questions. She asks questions because they will save her from wasting time. The average woman learns particular facts *after* she has invested her body, soul, and spirit. But a queen will determine the disconnect through questioning long before she is invested.

> *The Bible encourages us to not be unequally yoked together, which means that we should not join ourselves to those who are fundamentally incompatible.*

The Apostle Paul admonished the Corinthian church to be intentional about their relationships and not to be unequally yoked. The idea is to determine whether a relationship will work before you get into it, not ten years later.

The primary means of predetermining compatibility with another person is knowledge. The wise queen attains the necessary information that gives her the power to make educated decisions in relationships. She does not throw herself into a relationship and then hope for the best; rather, she interrogates and analyzes to ensure that there is a real basis for moving forward.

> *Wherever knowledge will flow, it must be primed by the pump of inquisition.*

The most legitimate reason certain men may be intimidated by queens is that they cannot stand under the pressure of the questioning. A queen will ask a question and look a man directly in the eyes to see into his heart rather than just hearing his words.

QUESTIONS ONLY A QUEEN WOULD ASK

"What matters most to you in life?"
A queen gets directly to the heart of the matter. She will ask a man, in no uncertain terms, "What are your priorities?" The way a person answers this question will immediately reveal whether there is any genuine, common ideological and or philosophical basis for connecting. If the queen is a "go get it" visionary and the man has to think long and hard to produce an answer to such a direct question, she knows instantly that they have no connection.

A list of a person's priorities reveals the truest nature of their heart. It tells if they are shallow or substantive. The Bible puts it this way in Matthew 6:21, *For where your treasure is, there will your heart be also.* The reference to treasure speaks of a person's interest, priorities, and the things a person values. Once we locate where a person's invested interest is, we maintain a position on that person's heart.

> **The queen should ask this question abruptly so that a contrived answer may not be fabricated.**

When the queen poses her questions, she also uses timing to disrupt the capacity to deceive. The queen drops these questions at the most unexpected times to get the most authentic responses. The queen may go from a conversation concerning pets and sports and shift abruptly to, "What is most important to you in your life?"

"What attracted you to me?"
This is a question that average women do not ask, or if they do, they hope for a typical superficial reply, appeasing them by an answer as shallow as, "You are the most beautiful woman in the world." A queen needs more than

a flesh-level connection with a potential king. He has to see her beneath the surface.

> *A queen needs to hear references to her heart, her drive, her vision, her intellect. These are the aspects of life that are enduring, and are the foundation of strong lifelong connections.*

If the man's attraction does not reach into the subsurface regions of the queen's life, she should proceed with great caution.

The woman should ask a man what attracts him to her early in their conversations. A queen needs to know the source of this man's interest. Knowing what he's attracted to will reveal if the connection has covenant potential (marriage) or just another opportunity for pointless copulation (sex).

> *If a man is not attracted to the right parts of a woman, he is not her king.*

"What is your vision?"
A queen makes her relationship decisions by things greater than hormonal stimulation or some fleeting sexual impulse. She has authority, influence, and power. Any man who lies next to a queen has to possess the vision to see things bigger and better than they presently are. A queen will never have a man who has no vision.

> *A man without a vision is a bore to a queen.*

The queen will always ask a man to define his vision. It is

by the depth of his vision that the queen may make certain determinations. His vision will let her know if he is
intellectually comparable. It reveals whether he is truly
enough of a leader for her to follow.

> *A man without a vision has no need*
> *for a queen. A queen is a gift to a king*
> *because she gives life to his vision.*

Adam was gifted with Eve because he had so much to
accomplish. It was only after Adam had a clear and distinct purpose that God said, *It is not good that man should
be alone; I will make him an help meet for him* (Genesis
2:18). If Adam did not have a vision, he would not have
needed help.

> *A queen is a gift to a king who needs*
> *help to accomplish dominion.*

If a man has no intention to dominate, he does not qualify for a queen. A queen should never take a man in as a
project. As powerful as a queen is, she does not have the
ability to make a blind man see.

"What is your spiritual foundation?"

A queen will absolutely have to know the spiritual life
of a man. A queen is not going to submit herself to a man
who will put her at odds with her God. She is not going
to allow the relationship to go anywhere until she is certain that she and the man are on the same spiritual page.

The word of God says in Colossians 3:18, *Wives, submit
yourselves unto your own husbands, as it is fit in the Lord.*
The submission part would be quite complicated if the

man is not in the Lord. A queen has to know the spiritual realities of a would-be king in her life.

The queen will ask this question at a time when she has the man's full attention. The questioning has to go to the extent that she is satisfied his answers represent his heart.

> *No queen will submit to a king who*
> *has not submitted to God.*

"What have you learned about me?"

Another line of questioning the queen may present is to ask the man to be specific about the things he's learned about her. Of course, this would have to come after some weeks, at least, of conversing and spending time together.

The reason this question is important is because a queen cannot be eternally content with a man who does not value her enough to pay attention to her. He should know her likes and dislikes.

> *A man who does not have specific answers to*
> *a woman's preferences either does not love her*
> *enough to care or is not smart enough to learn.*

1 Peter 3:7 instructs would be husbands to know their wives: *"Likewise, ye husbands, dwell with them according to knowledge, giving honour . . ."*

When a man really loves a woman, he learns her. A queen will not settle for a man who is clueless about her.

CHAPTER 8

QUEENS KEEP A ROYAL CIRCLE

QUEEN-CONSCIOUSNESS
(A Queen's Circle Has to Be Vetted Carefully)

As the young princesses became young women under the tutelage of their father, King Paternam, they became wiser and more self-conscious.

The king began to share his final wisdom for royal women. He talked about how there would be many people who would want to attach themselves to the princesses for their own selfish agendas. The king reminded them of the years they grew up as children in the care of subjects who were supposed to be friends to the royal family. He reminded them that these very people were the ones who manipulated them into believing that they were mere peasants, not rightful heirs. It was the so-called "friends" who betrayed the family.

The king shared with the young queens that a queen's circle has to be vetted. It must be tested and proven. Her circle cannot be haphazard, it must be intentional. He talked about the fact that their blessings also carried the burdens of betrayal, jealousy, and abandonment. A true queen can withstand all of these assaults and continue to rule. The one thing she must always do is periodically sanitize her circle.

I watch a lot of historical television shows—anything pertaining to royals and monarchs captivates me. One of the things that is consistent from one royal family, or era, to the next is isolation. Royals do not allow everybody or just anyone to gain access to their inner circle. Not everyone can come into the chambers. In fact, not all people were even allowed into the court. If people came to court without invitation, they could be executed. There were levels of access based on the individual's role in the king or queen's life.

Elevation never happens without detachment and isolation.

History has proven that royals who had a relaxed policy regarding access to their inner circle were either betrayed, assassinated, or debunked by intimate enemies. An intimate enemy rides with you, but aren't really rolling with you. They are on your ship, but they are in the rear drilling holes. In a more mainstream vernacular, they are people who pretend to be friends to simply access your resources and influence until they get where they want to be. After they've arrived, they may do a few unscrupulous things: They may set you up for destruction, as Brutus did to Caesar. They could abandon you without explanation, as Jesus' disciples did, or they could just use their documented proximity to validate a false depiction of your character to society.

A queen does not have time to fight the world. A wise queen will walk alone until she has definitely and completely proven her closest confidants.

A real queen does not entertain a random circle filled with unscrupulous characters.

A queen must understand the implications of association—by associating with certain people, she is simultaneously sharing her influence and power. Those influenced by the queen will automatically associate a due respect to all who are in the queen's circle. Also, the queen is allowing the other person or people to attach their social reputation to hers. Thus, if something goes wrong, the queen is automatically judged in the court of public opinion as being guilty by association. A queen can't walk in close fellowship with gold diggers and maintain the persona of an honorable woman. Sometimes the queen is sincerely trying to bring everybody from her past into her future, so she becomes a die-hard about holding on to old relationships that clearly don't agree with her future.

Some relationships have an expiration date.

The most negative consequence of a poor circle around a queen is that she adopts some of the bad habits and character flaws of those who are constantly interfacing with her. As my father, Bishop Robert Blakes, Sr., would have said, "If you lie down with dirty dogs, you're certain to wake up with fleas."

The word of God puts it like this in 1 Corinthians 15:33, *Be not deceived: evil communications corrupt good manners.* The term communication speaks of more than conversation—it means an ongoing fellowship with a person.

When a queen is influenced daily by
a common person, it will eventually
dilute her regal standards.

People must be periodically repositioned, replaced, or sometimes removed. It is what it is. When it's time to make adjustments to your circle, you must make the best decision for you. I am a living witness that allowing your heart to delay a decision your head should have been authorized to make can break your heart, delay your vision, and impact your bank account.

> **When it is clearly time for people
> to go, you must shift swiftly.**

The Bible records the life of Abram and all of the promises that God made to him. The one stipulation God set forth was that Abram was to go and search for a prosperous land that God would reveal. The interesting thing is that God told Abram not to bring his family. What did Abram do? He brought his family. As the story unfolds, his family caused him to get into wars he was never supposed to fight. He had contention and drama that he should have never experienced, and he had to relinquish a part of his wealth to ultimately get rid of his kinsman by the name of Lot (Genesis 13:1-12).

The interesting thing is that after Abram gives Lot whatever parts of the land he wanted as a concession for him to depart, God started talking to Abram again. This is recorded in Genesis 13:14-15:

> *And the Lord said unto Abram, after that Lot was separated from him, Lift up now thine eyes, and look from the place where thou art northward, and southward, and eastward, and westward:*
>
> *For all the land that thou seest, to thee I will give it, and to thy seed for ever.*

Sometimes a queen is restricting the favor of God
because she refuses to bury dead relationships.

These relationships may be dead friendships or love affairs that are on life support. Whatever prevents you from hearing God's voice clearly has to go.

As queen, you must sanitize your circle.

As we study the ways of queens, we absolutely have to remember the life of Queen Esther. Esther is the ultimate depiction of a queen—she was a queen from her heart to her headdress. Esther had the looks, brains, character, and heart of a queen.

If you read the story of Queen Esther, you'll discover that she had a preparation period before she was made queen. She had to be isolated to a circle of ladies who shared her same royal potential. When Esther was selected as a potential queen, she was required to separate from the general population and to limit her contacts and connections to women who shared her potential. This is recorded in Esther 2:8:

> *So when the king's command and his decree*
> *were proclaimed and when many maidens*
> *were gathered in Shushan the capital under the*
> *custody of Hegai, Esther also was taken to the*
> *king's house into the custody of Hegai, keeper*
> *of the women* (AMPC).

Esther had to be sanctified (set apart). Queens today must accept the concept of isolation. You will have to purge certain people from your life to live the life God has in store for you.

One of the gravest mistakes is to take the wrong
people into the most delicate spaces of your life.

Esther's circle had to be sanitized. It had to be purged. I'm afraid that most queens abandon their thrones when it comes to this point. Many queens are so enmeshed to the people of their past and present, they are unwilling to release them to go victoriously into their future.

One of the toughest actions a queen makes is to sanitize her circle of people who are firmly etched in her history, but serve no part in her destiny.

Maintaining relationships that do not represent your future or philosophy only cements you into your current status. You will never move beyond this point. Detoxing from people may be the single greatest maneuver a queen will have to make to advance her life.

The world will see you through the lens of your circle.

You are eventually categorized by the company you keep. If you were to take a Mercedes and put it in the middle of a fleet of Toyotas, it would take on the same semblance of a Toyota.

A queen protects her image and never allows herself to be compromised by other people's baggage.

So many sisters are sabotaged by poor company. They take on associates and acquaintances that only hold them back and taint their image. One of the great distinctions between common-consciousness and queen-conscious-ness is the capacity to eliminate. A queen is not addicted to futile relationships, she desires intentional relationships.

For her, holding her position down requires knowing how to walk alone when necessary.

A queen values her name and reputation
too much to surround herself with
questionable characters.

The circle you maintain either encourages progression or regression. A queen recognizes that she needs ongoing growth. Most of the development and continued education of a person comes from her circle.

The people that surround you will push you into your tomorrow or marry you to yesterday. Your friend that was the master of cassette tapes in the 80s may not serve you too well in the MP3 download generation. Every level will dismiss certain old people and introduce new people.

A queen has many decisions to make and realizes
the absolute necessity of having a smart circle.

Periodically, a queen has to purge her circle of those who do not add to her knowledge base or wisdom. Her court must be filled with people who are often smarter than she is in particular areas.

If you are the smartest person in your circle, you
are really the dumbest—you are the only one not
smart enough to have someone to glean from.

What is the point of maintaining relationships that do not add to your knowledge base? Why spend three or four days a week and hours on the phone with people who do not inspire new thoughts or concepts? If you are spending all of your time with people who do not know as much as you, your circle needs to be sanitized.

Not everyone will be purged; some will simply be repositioned into another category. As you take inventory of your relationships, you will discover that some are adding nothing to your life and have an agenda that no longer serves your interest. These people must be graciously dismissed from your life. On the other hand, there are some who may not be the best fit for your life at the moment, but they share your drive and they love you sincerely—these people should be wisely repositioned into some area of your life. Never lose those who have a sincere love for you, just reassign them to a place that suits them and doesn't hinder your reign.

SEVEN ASPECTS OF A QUEEN'S INNER CIRCLE

1. A Queen's Circle Must Be Loyal to Her.
You should never embrace a person to serve in your inner circle who is best friends with your chief enemy. Of course, it is possible for your friend to be cordial with your enemy, but they will never be able to embrace your enemy as a best friend if they are truly loyal to you.

There is a beautiful story of the loyalty an older woman's daughter-in-law had for her mother-in-law after her husband, the woman's son, had died. It is the story of Ruth and Naomi, found in Ruth 1:16-17:

> And Ruth said, Intreat me not to leave thee, or to return from following after thee: for whither thou goest, I will go; and where thou lodgest I will lodge: thy people shall be my people, and thy God my God:

*Where thou diest, will I die, and there will I be
buried: the Lord do so to me, and more also, if
ought but death part thee and me.*

Here we see the embodiment of loyalty: It is a choice to be with another. It is never based on advantages or compensation, it is based on an undeniable love for the person. It is articulated and constantly demonstrated. Ruth made it very plain she was going to be with Naomi under any conditions.

A queen doesn't need a big
circle, just a loyal circle.

A loyal circle of people will hold you up when you're down and support you when the world is doing its best to pull you down when you're up. God will give you people who will fight to the bitter end. You do not get many such people in a normal lifetime.

The word of God says in Proverbs 18:24, *A man that hath friends must shew himself friendly: and there is a friend that sticketh closer than a brother.*

2. A Queen's Circle Must Be Honorable and Honest.

A queen must never have shady characters in her inner circle. She will have access to great resources and influential people, but when your circle is filled with dishonorable people, they will take advantage of your favor and possibly burn vital bridges behind your back.

The prophet Elisha experienced this with his servant Gehazi. There was a man by the name of Naamar, who came to the prophet to be healed of leprosy. After God miraculously healed his leprosy, Naaman wanted to give the prophet some money. Elisha refused and sent him on his way. In the meantime, Gehazi heard this conversation because he was in the inner circle. Gehazi ran after Naaman and told him that the prophet changed his mind and would receive compensation. So Gehazi took the money in the name of Elisha. Of course, God revealed Gehazi's actions to Elisha and Elisha called the same leprosy that was on Naaman onto Gehazi. (The record of this story is found in 2 Kings 5:1-27.)

Elisha's servant Gehazi lacked integrity and honor. However, if he were not in the inner circle, he would not have had an opportunity to embarrass and misrepresent the man of God.

3. A Queen's Circle Must Provide Wise Counsel.

So many women with unbelievable potential unnecessarily squander it because they took counsel from the wrong people. A counselor has to possess certain factors. She must be genuinely invested in your wellbeing and have some knowledge or insight that may be useful in pushing you to the next level. Finally, she must have enough love to counsel you as well as the wisdom to know how and when.

> *A counselor is not a controller—a counselor*
> *is a GPS system to your goals.*

There's a man in the Bible who was very important, but he had a condition that jeopardized his very life. If he had not received very wise counsel from someone who loved him, he would have died. The counsel he needed came from a servant, but this servant was in the inner circle. He possessed wisdom and he loved the man enough to steer him right. This was the encounter of Naaman and one of his servants . . . Naaman's servant is the one who steered him to Elisha and healing. (The story is found in 2 Kings 5:8-14.)

> *Everybody who loves you is not qualified*
> *to counsel you, but those that would*
> *counsel you definitely love you.*

Counsel in your inner circle keeps you safe from calamity and unnecessary problems.

4. A Queen's Circle Must Celebrate Her Victories as Their Own.

Why do you continue to work on relationships with false sisters who are obviously jealous of you? Why? It is a massive waste of time. No one should have intimate access to your life that is the least bit jealous of you. When you read the account of Jesus receiving the gift of oil from the alabaster box, you see that Judas gets offended at the value of the oil being poured upon Jesus. It is right after he gets jealous of Jesus' gift that he goes out to make the deal to betray Jesus. (The record of this incident is found in Matthew 26:6-16.)

> *Anyone who cannot rejoice in your*
> *blessing is not a true friend.*

The Bible says in Romans 12:15, *Rejoice with them that do rejoice, and weep with them that weep.*

Who do you have in your life that genuinely rejoices with you in your victories? A true friend is never jealous of you. In fact, they actually get more excited about your good favor than you do.

The clearest example of this type of inner circle relationship would be Jonathan and David. Jonathan always celebrated David's success. He was never envious of the Lord's choosing David to reign over Israel, even though Jonathan was the biological heir apparent.

> *Anybody who can't celebrate*
> *you may assassinate you.*

The wise man Solomon puts it this way in Proverbs 6:34, *For jealousy is the rage of a man: therefore he will not spare in the day of vengeance.*

In other words, when a person is jealous of you, they will go to unbelievable extremes when they find an occasion to be angry with you. Keeping a jealous person close is like making a pet of a tiger—you never know when its base nature will destroy you.

5. A Queen's Circle Must Be Reliable.

You need people who keep their word in your inner circle. It's not enough to have people who are always meaning to come through but consistently find excuses for why they've failed you. A queen can lose valuable time depending on undependable people. Don't invite a headache into your life. Keep people around you that have a word and come through more times than not.

The Bible puts it this way in Psalm 15:4, *In whose eyes a vile person is despised, but he who honors those who fear the Lord (who revere and worship him); who swears to his own hurt and does not change* (AMPC).

Wow! Do you see how Psalm 15:4 ends? A person who is worthy of the inner circle is one who will give their word and take a personal loss before they disappoint you.

Of course, this especially applies to any would-be king in the queen's life. Who needs a king that cannot be counted on? If he has more excuses than a brother in jail, he must be banished.

Never tolerate close relationships that rarely deliver. Friends that let you down should at least be repositioned. Even family members who are not consistent and dependable must not be allowed to constantly circumvent your rise by disappointing your expectations and their commitments to you.

The Bible also says in Proverbs 25:19, *Confidence in an unfaithful man in time of trouble is like a broken tooth, and a foot out of joint.*

6. A Queen's Circle Must Provide Inspiration.

To inspire means to be put "in spirit." A person who inspires you awakens you spiritually and emotionally. When a queen has fought systems and has sharpened her skill set, she needs to retreat to people who bring her up and minister to her as she ministers to them. Life is too short and challenging to walk with people who do not bring your spirit up.

> *If a person does not make you excited*
> *about your life, they shouldn't be in*
> *an intimate place in your life.*

They may not mean any harm, but they will do a lot of damage if they don't care enough to learn what restores you. Don't surround yourself with faith-killers and joy-drainers. Fill your team up with people who make you believe you can win!

For instance, you will discover that most people will bring you one problem after another. Every day they will invent a problem to present to you. On the flip side, there are other people who only want to make your load lighter and they intentionally work to put you in a relaxed state of mind.

In fact, Jesus had this same issue with two of his friends, as Luke 10:38-42 tells it:

> Now it came to pass, as they went, that he entered into a certain village: and a certain woman named Martha received him into her house.
>
> And she had a sister called Mary, which sat at Jesus' feet, and heard his word.
>
> But Martha was cumbered about much serving, and came to him, and said, Lord, doth thou not care that my sister hath left me to serve alone? bid her therefore that she help me.
>
> And Jesus answered and said unto her Martha, Martha, thou art careful and troubled about many things:
>
> But one thing is needful: and Mary hath chosen that good part, which shall not be taken away from her.

This is a record of two sisters who had very different approaches to their personal relationship with Jesus. One sister, Martha, was so consumed with chores that she did not make Jesus her priority. Maybe in her own mind and way, she thought she was. The other sister,

Mary, immediately sat at his feet and made him her focal point. This ministered to Jesus' spirit. When Martha began to complain, Jesus rebuked Martha and encouraged Mary to continue what she was doing.

> *Every queen deserves to have people in her life*
> *who will replenish the energy the world extracts.*

Never load your wagon down with people who have a Martha mentality and can only see tasks, but never see you.

7. A Queen's Circle Fights for Her.

Every woman needs the support of people who will have her back when she's not looking. Everybody has your back when they are in your face, but who has your back when you can't see them? Some people have these so-called friends who talk a big love game, but they never get into the battle. When you are going through your most difficult financial season, who chips in? When you are having health challenges that are rocking you to your core, who sits in the hospital with you? When you have physical enemies, who is ready to take up arms to defend you?

> *You do not need people in your inner*
> *circle who won't fight for you.*

Here's some more wisdom from the proverbs of Solomon, found in Proverbs 17:17: *A friend loveth at all times, and a brother is born for adversity.*

Every queen needs friends who love her through every situation and do not fail her during adversity.

CONCLUSION

It is my hope that something has been awakened in you. My prayer is that the words of this book have created a personal encounter for you . . . with the real you. Too many queens drift through life totally unaware of their true station. You are the prize of God's creation! Many have done well, but you, my dear, will excel them all.

Keep your mind focused, your circle royal, and your ambitions high. You are queen. It does not matter how much you've had to come through to get here—you have arrived. Your destiny is sure. God will perfect everything He's created you for. Believe that!

Do not doubt your ability to complete the rest of your journey. Every setback and scar is a reminder that you are stronger than you give yourself credit for. You are made of royal stock, and there is no challenge that is equal to you.

Don't allow the world to sell you cheap! Know your worth and demand what you deserve. Always remember to walk with equals. There's a reason pigeons and eagles don't fly together.

You are queen despite your pain. You are queen despite your path. You are queen despite your mistakes.

YOU ARE QUEEN!
BE QUEEN.

Epilogue

QUEEN-CONSCIOUSNESS
(King Paternam and the Three Princesses)

As the years passed and the girls matured, King Paternam poured all of his wisdom into them. The king got the kingdom back to a place of peace and prosperity, but more importantly, he installed the royal mindset of queens into his young princesses. His legacy was secure. He would live on through his girls and they would be the strong rulers they were born to be.

Each of the girls perfected her own particular strength, but all three manifested a grace and balance that set them apart from average women of the kingdom. It was clear that they were cut from a different cloth as they moved about the kingdom, and King Paternam was proud of his young queens.

The girls had embodied the nature and psychology of queens. As the king gazed upon them, he saw the rebirth of their dear mother, his late queen.

The girls walked throughout the kingdom with wisdom, discretion, judgement, grace, humility, and power. The young women were the envy of all nations. Kings from other nations were calling to pursue the young, strong, and wise queens to wed them. But the princesses took their time making decisions about relationships because King Paternam had *instilled in the girls the value of never hurrying to answer a king in pursuit.*

Potestatum dedicated herself to the mastery of economics. She brought about a great era of prosperity to the kingdom.

Honestum cared greatly for the poor. She created a national charity outreach and developed a national program to empower the poor for employment and earn a living wage.

Imperium took to the ways of politics. She introduced policies at court that revolutionized her father's kingdom.

All were not pleased that the king liberated his daughters to function in traditionally male capacities, but no one dared to challenge them. The young princesses were as sharp as any man and as strong as their father. They had become queens in their own right.

Eventually, the girls all wed great kings from neighboring kingdoms. They brought their version of Queendom to the various kingdoms. Their husbands were deeply in love with each of them, for they were women that excelled all others.

In each of their respective kingdoms there was a new curriculum required for young women. It was called "QUEENOLOGY: The Study of Queens". From their realms, generations of women who understood their power and demanded their worth changed the world.

King Paternam lived to be a very old man. He had great relationships with his sons-in-law. The girls had many children, and the king lived to see even his great-grandchildren rule. The various kingdoms of the family created a union, and the realm became impregnable. It was the wealthiest and strongest union on the planet. So the king, his girls, and their families lived happily ever after.

The End